THE PLAN

THE PLAN

PAT ROBERTSON

THOMAS NELSON PUBLISHERS
Nashville

Contents

The Lord of Hosts has sworn, saying,
"Surely, as I have thought, so it
shall come to pass,
And as I have purposed,
so it shall stand."

Isaiah 14:24

THE PLAN

Preface

New Orleans is hot and steamy in the summertime, and the summer of 1988 was no exception. But those of us attending the presidential nominating convention of the Republican party in August of 1988 weren't concerned about the weather.

We had come to nominate the next president of the United States, to position our candidates to win in the fall, to alternately appeal to or strong-arm our way through armies of reporters, and to draft a platform which represented strong conservative patriotic family values.

To many of the assembled delegates and alternates— and there were almost five thousand of them—this was a time to revel in the closest brush with real political power they might ever know, while taking time to taste the delights of what many feel is the best party town in America.

For me, convention week in New Orleans in August was to be bittersweet. I had run as a candidate for the Republican nomination for the presidency. I had run hard and, in the process, had raised the hopes and dreams of hundreds of thousands of Americans who shared my goal of "restoring the greatness of America through moral strength."

They had worked sacrificially, tirelessly, enthusiastically. They had given millions of dollars. They had proved in state after state that God-fearing, dedicated people, even though novices, when working for a cause, can get into politics and win.

They had shocked the political world in the early maneuvering by scoring a resounding victory in Michigan. Then in the crucial preliminary straw balloting in Iowa—which had broken Jimmy Carter out of the pack in 1975—they beat all the candidates and gave me a resounding victory over a sitting vice president and the minority leader of the United States senate. Excluding Michigan, which, frankly, was stolen from them, they had won four states, scored second in about eight more, and had brought me a third place finish out of a field of six with 1.9 million votes.

In the quest for the highest secular prize our nation has to offer, a third place finish is respectable. But my supporters were devastated. It was as if they mourned for the dead. Because they felt—as I did—that God had called me to win, not run third.

So in New Orleans they were asking and I was asking one simple question—did God call me to run for president or not? And if He did call me to run, why did I lose? And why, with the loss, was there such incredible personal abuse and such enormous financial sacrifice?

Did God have a plan for me? Does He have a plan for you? Can you and I learn God's plan for our lives, so that we will have lives filled with purpose and meaning, joy and satisfaction? This book will tell you the secrets of knowing God's plan for you.

PART ONE

---

*Does God Have
A Plan for Your Life?*

1

Did I Miss It?

This is thrilling, but . . .

Those words were there, even as I walked to the front of the monstrous platform. The roar was thunderous. The placards surged and waved wildly. The banners fluttered. The band screeched in and out of the roar.

Those words, unspoken, continued: *I'm being treated like a winner . . . but I didn't win.*

The New Orleans Superdome is gigantic. The stands surrounding the arena can hold eighty-nine thousand cheering fans, gathered to watch a Super Bowl game being played on the astro turf floor. Now that floor was filled with five thousand delegates and alternates, neatly arranged in rows, which radiated like spokes from where I was standing on the two-story, flag-decked platform, crowned by a super electronic billboard.

In front of the speakers' platform, mounted at eye level on an equally imposing platform, were the cameras from three broadcast networks, Cable News Network, and the in-house television system. Surrounding the upper reaches of the domed stadium were the sky boxes of the media where Dan Rather, Tom Brokaw, Peter Jennings, and David Brinkley would pontificate for hours on what they felt were the enduring truths of the Republican Convention.

Fred Malek, the gentle business great, who had come to the party from the presidency of the Marriott Hotel chain, was masterminding the entire proceeding for maximum appeal to the nation's television viewers. No detail had been omitted—even the height of individual speakers. The floor behind the podium was built for a six-foot, one-inch man. Each participant stood on a moveable hydraulic platform. By the press of a button, short speakers grew to six-feet, one-inches in height and by the press of another button tall speakers shrank to six-feet one.

The convention leadership had wanted nothing to mar the sense of unity needed for success. All four of the leading candidates had been given a key speaking role in reverse order of their finish in the primaries. Jack Kemp would speak on Monday, my time was after the keynote on Tuesday, Bob Dole was given Wednesday, and the grand finale on Thursday was reserved for the winner: George Bush.

Each evening had been carefully crafted. Each speech had been reviewed, timed, and edited by a panel of experts, including former White House speech writers. Each speech had been rehearsed in advance on teleprompter before an expert speech coach. It was a multi-million dollar extravaganza worthy of Cecil B. DeMille or Mike Todd.

Public opinion polls bore eloquent testimony to the skills of Malek and his staff. George Bush went into New Orleans an alarming eighteen points behind the Democratic nominee, Michael Dukakis. He came out of the convention nine points ahead. The candidate broke through to the American people, who in one week moved an incredible 27 percent in their preference!

I had been assigned a major speech—seventeen minutes of text and five minutes for a demonstration.

But what kind of demonstration?

What would make four thousand Bush people carry Robertson placards for the five minutes the convention had allocated to me? Our convention director, Marlene Elwell, the Roman Catholic political genius who served so well as my campaign manager in both Michigan and Iowa, had the solution. Our convention signs would scream in bold letters: "ROBERTSON FOR BUSH."

Her plan worked. Rich Bond, the Bush floor whip, approved the concept. That Tuesday evening, a copy of my book *America's Dates with Destiny* was on every delegate's chair. Under every chair was a placard in blue and white: "ROBERTSON FOR BUSH."

I am an experienced speaker with years before television cameras and large audiences. The speech was mine. I had worked it and reworked it. Those square, clear plastic devices you may have noticed in front of the speakers' podium were actually reflecting teleprompters. I knew every word would be there in bold type when I needed it.

With all that, I was still nervous. I also knew I was facing a skeptical, if not hostile audience, and a press corps which experience had taught me could be insulting and vicious.

During my speech that night I realized that I was being privileged to define for the leadership of the assembled

Republican party what we believed as Republicans: the sanctity of human life, fiscal sanity, lower taxes, the rollback of intrusive government programs, and our revulsion at ACLU liberals who let criminals go free while innocent citizens cowered in fear. Political analyst Garry Wills apparently realized the same thing when he wrote in the post-election issue of *Time* magazine that George Bush won the election because he "adopted Pat Robertson's cause." According to Wills, "Robertson issued the marching orders [for the campaign] in his speech at the New Orleans Convention."[1]

My speech was not intended as "marching orders," but as the words of a soldier bringing up a division of troops to support the corps commander.

"Hope is very much alive in America today," I concluded. "It is alive because our vision, the Republican vision, expresses the hopes and the dreams of the vast majority of the American people.

"And as we leave New Orleans, we will go back to our homes confident that we are a party united around a platform that expresses the American spirit—a platform we can be proud to share with our neighbors all over this great nation.

"Now . . ." My voice dropped slightly. My eyes went for a split second to the podium and then back to the mass of smiling faces. ". . . I would like to give a personal, special message to the millions of voters, volunteers, and supporters across America who committed themselves to my campaign."

I fixed my eyes on the upturned faces in front of the platform. "I thank you. I am very proud of you."

The roar broke out again. I could only smile and wonder. I continued: "This party is about to nominate a man that I have come to respect and admire. This man can and will lead our nation proudly into the future.

"Therefore, tonight I release my delegates and alternates who have come to this convention and urge you and all of my friends across America to give your enthusiastic support to our party, our candidates, and our presidential nominee."

I knew the closing lines well. "As we cast our eyes toward November, we know that a new page of history will be written. On that page we will inscribe the name of the forty-first president of the United States. His name will be George Bush, Republican."

The roar began to rise again. "Thank you and God bless you!"

Pandemonium broke out as I moved two short steps backward, raised my left hand high, and waved it slowly. The parading resumed in the aisles. The band strove valiantly to be heard. The placards waved.

Straight ahead I could see the green-and-white umbrellas of the Robertson delegation from the state of Washington. To the left of them, in the midst of a cheering Virginia delegation, a congressman was standing on a chair, tears streaming down his face, waving a handkerchief over his head. Hundreds of old friends and thousands of new ones cheered and waved "ROBERTSON FOR BUSH" placards.

My wife, Dede, joined me on the platform. I put my arm around her waist and we waved, and smiled, and cheered inwardly. But soon the five minutes were over, the band stopped playing, and we exited the platform. Then a couple of interviews, a walk to our vehicle through a rapidly emptying auditorium, and my 1988 presidential campaign was over.

Was the Decision Wrong?

I remember well the end of the summer of 1984 when numerous conservative, highly-placed friends came to ask me about my running for public office. "We need—the country needs—somebody like you to run for office, and we'd like to see you run for President."

My reaction was immediate. "There is no way I'd run against Ronald Reagan," who would be seeking and winning a second term. "I wouldn't even entertain such a notion. And furthermore, I like the job I have. It provides a pretty good platform for addressing the needs of the country. I'm not sure public office would be a promotion."

I loved my work. The Christian Broadcasting Network (CBN) had grown from a seventy-dollar beginning to a multifaceted enterprise that included the nation's fifth largest cable television network. CBN University is a fully accredited graduate institution with five colleges, including a law school. CBN also has a major private sector relief agency called Operation Blessing; a highly effective literacy program, "Sing, Spell, Read and Write"; international broadcast operations and relief centers serving millions in twenty-seven nations; and 700 Club Crisis Counseling Centers responding to more than two million calls for help each year. I felt I could do more good there than anywhere else, including the presidency of the greatest nation in the world.

Still, the inquiries persisted—telephone calls, visits, private conversations at conferences. I listened, but I really wasn't impressed.

It was four or five weeks later that I found myself focusing on the subject during times of prayer and Bible readings. The possibility of such a step came into my mind more and more.

Then came early October and what we call "Seven Days Ablaze," our annual time of prayer and fasting, coinciding with the Jewish New Year, Rosh Hashana, and Succoth, the Feast of Tabernacles. As I set aside several days for earnest prayer, I was startled when an impression came into my mind: *You will not want to do this, but you should do it.*

I really didn't want to accept that. It was easy to rationalize that such an impression had come through some quirky mental process, some power-of-suggestion. But it came back again and again over several weeks.

As I prayed, I went from "This can't be right, Lord" to "Please don't let me be misled about this." I knew the still voice of the Lord. It persisted and deepened. Over and over, *You won't want to do this, but. . . .*

Of course, ideas about government and politics weren't new to me. My father went to the House of Representatives when I was two and then to the Senate when I was sixteen. I had been raised on politics, and while I was in law school worked for a summer on the staff of the Senate Appropriations Committee. My real interest in public policy was jolted into action in 1981 when, for the first time, I truly realized the enormity of the plan of the ACLU, the N.E.A., and Planned Parenthood to destroy Christian values in America. Freedom after freedom was being taken away: prayer in the schools, Bible reading, Bible clubs, Christmas activities and displays. Christians needed an organization to counter this unbelievable loss of our liberty. That year I formed the Freedom Council to educate Evangelical Christians on the vital issues and then to get them into the public process. I also set up the National Legal Foundation to fight the ACLU in the courts. I was not only well-acquainted with most of the issues of current political life, I had become a national champion of evangelical rights. Still, couldn't I do more good as a leader of a national network plus a grass roots organization than I could by personally becoming a political candidate?

As I prayed about this decision, the answer was increasingly, *No*. That was coupled with an awareness that I could hardly ask others to do something I was unwilling to do.

I prayed daily about it. One question repeated to God time after time was simply: "Is this Your will for me?" Then a humble plea, "Father, don't let me be misled!"

My chief concern was about leaving CBN. I knew that if God was leading me to run for the presidency, God would also have someone to take care of CBN. The only issue was what did He want? I knew that God could make His will clear to His people. He had certainly done so to me, time and time again. Now that same gentle leading I had known for over thirty years was with me—a still voice, a passage in the Bible, the peace in my heart, the word of a friend. All like signposts pointing the way.

During the Seven Days Ablaze of 1984 I felt especially close to the Lord. It seemed that I could ask for and receive anything from Him. What I really wanted was clear direction about His plan for my life. So I decided to check my spiritual pulse by a specific prayer request.

Since 1978 I had wanted a larger jet-powered airplane for CBN to accomplish our mission. I am noted for frugality and there was no way I would consider paying $3 million to $4.5 million for such planes (the BAC1–11's). Sitting on the terrace on that sun-drenched October day, I looked up to heaven and simply said, "If I am hearing from You, Father, please give us a BAC1–11 airplane." I wanted it for free or so cheap that it seemed to be free.

My answer came in February of 1985 when we acquired a beautiful BAC1–11 for a price so cheap that it was almost equal to the cost of a recent overhaul of its engines. This jet was big enough to easily carry television crews, equipment, staff members, and quantities of literature.

This seemed a sign that I was in touch with God. Many more were to follow. After the primaries were over my question "Is this Your will?" became "Did I miss Your leading, Father?"

Did I Miss God?

I've been asked the question a hundred times: "Did you miss God?" I asked over and over, "Did I miss Your leading,

Father? Did You lead me? Did I hear You? Was this the wrong thing? Why didn't I win?"

The questions were not easy ones. I knew absolutely that I had received clearer, stronger guidance to run for the Republican nomination for president of the United States than I had received when I was unmistakably directed by the Lord to go to Virginia in 1959 and start a television ministry. But why, if God was leading me, had I been defeated? Why had I been so battered, smeared, and humiliated? Why had my family been so abused? Why had so many other people been hurt? Why had the work of my life, The Christian Broadcasting Network and its related activities, been so badly damaged.

These thoughts were there in New Orleans that 1988 convention night when I was greeted and applauded and thanked, but nonetheless went home as an also-ran. They were the thoughts that tormented me and those close to me, back in Virginia Beach as I gave my attention once again to CBN. These thoughts were there when I asked God why He permitted the unjust castigation and vilification that I had received from the press.

Did God have a plan for me? Did I miss it by running for president? Is it possible for you to know God's will and guidance in the large and small matters of life? Indeed, does God have a will—a plan—for individuals and nations and the church? How can we keep from missing God's plan for us?

This book explores these questions and shares the details of answers, perspectives, and experiences from which all of us can learn. Yes, God has a plan for our lives.

Yes, we can know that plan and live in it. We can take heart in the historic fact that God is concerned with the eternal and with the temporal. In the final analysis, they are one.

2

You Are Somebody

In 1978, I lived on the outskirts of Suffolk, Virginia, in a rented antebellum farm house with four big square columns on the porch, a huge magnolia tree in the front yard, and a tidal marsh in back fed by a stream called Streeter Creek, which emptied about a half mile downstream into the James River, not far from the mouth of the Chesapeake Bay.

I was isolated by a thousand acres of rolling farmland, a blessed provision from God through a wealthy benefactor, Fred Beazley. Through the front window was the stately magnolia tree, then a white rail fence and beyond that a lush pasture. Through the side window a view of pine trees in a ravine leading to Streeter Creek, beyond them a field of soybeans.

The early morning hours were quiet and I made a practice of spending those quiet moments reading the Bible and praying.

One morning I was engrossed in a study of the book of Isaiah. Then something happened. The words of Isaiah the prophet came alive:

Is it not to share your bread with the hungry . . .
When you see the naked, that you cover him . . .

And that you bring to your house the poor who are
   cast out . . . ."[1]

I had read this many times, but it was Old Testament, I
thought, and not binding on us today. I read on:

Then your light shall break forth like the morning . . .
The glory of the LORD shall be your rear guard . . . .
Then you shall call, and the LORD will answer . . .
Your light shall dawn in the darkness . . .
The LORD will guide you continually![2]

Old Testament or not, these were the blessings I
wanted in my life: answered prayer, God's protection,
light on my life, and continual guidance.

Quickly, carefully, I listed all of my obligations and duties on one side of a yellow legal pad. Then on the other
side, I listed all of my blessings.

Here I was in a beautiful setting. I had moved there
from a near slum situation in downtown Portsmouth.
Could I enjoy all of this without remembering the poor
who lived where I used to live?

I had God's absolute word that if I would give of my life
to serve the physical needs of the poor and needy, God
would serve me with the things I wanted most in my life.
Above all else He would *guide me continually*.

Some words from the Lord don't need to be debated by
a committee. You can act on them now. This word was
clear. Unmistakable. What one of my vice presidents calls
a "no brainer."

I got dressed and drove in to our Portsmouth, Virginia,
television studio. "The 700 Club" program is broadcast

across the nation at ten o'clock each morning. We have twenty-four-hour counseling centers, but there are also centers all across America specially manned to take crisis counseling telephone calls while "The 700 Club" program is being aired. With only thirty minutes until air time, I told the national counseling director, "Alert your people. We are starting a new program today. It will be called 'Operation Blessing.'"

Then I went on national television and asked the people what they would exchange to have the most desirable blessings in all the world. On the blackboard I wrote down a complete list of all the blessings promised by Isaiah.

Then I said, "Here is the price," and I proceeded to list what God required of us in order to receive those blessings.

It seemed so simple. If someone was hungry, let someone else with food help him. If someone was short on clothes, let someone else with extra clothes help. If someone was elderly and couldn't drive, let someone who was able-bodied do the driving. If someone could not afford dental care, let a skilled dentist fix the teeth.

So I said, "If you have abilities, call our numbers. If you have needs, call our numbers. We will try to match needs with abilities all over America. Those who give will be blessed. Those who receive will be blessed." (Hence the name, "Operation Blessing.")

How could I have dreamed that in ten years Operation Blessing would grow into one of the biggest private relief agencies in America. That humble beginning resulted in the facilitation of direct grants from CBN plus community support of over $200 million sent all over the world. Over 30 million needy people have been either fed, clothed, housed, or educated throughout the United States.

Did God keep His promise in the book of Isaiah? You know the answer—of course, He did. Particularly that promise which says, "The Lord will guide you continually."[3]

Without question God will guide us. Most Americans believe that God has a plan for their lives, according to a recent Gallup Poll.

Eighty Percent Believe That God Has a Plan

The Gallup polling organization is without peer in America. Results of a Gallup Poll, with its acknowledged error factor of plus or minus 5 percent, usually are considered conclusive proof of the attitudes of the American people.

George Gallup, Jr., who heads this enterprise is a personal friend who has always been willing in his national polls to accommodate the need of CBN News to learn up-to-date trends in the religious attitudes of our nation.

What we discovered in this latest poll frankly amazed us. America is a very religious nation, much more so than any other industrialized nation in the world. Fully 94 percent of the American people believe in a supreme being and roughly 70 percent believe that Jesus Christ was the divine Son of God.[4]

Given the crass materialism we see in our land, it is even more surprising to learn that up to 80 percent of all the people in America believe that *God has a plan for their lives.*[5]

You see, despite the timeless attempt by educators to drill into our heads that we are all here by evolutionary accident, the American people aren't buying it. They refuse to believe that they are just bits of matter locked on an evolutionary ladder in an impersonal world. They know that they are creatures of God with a special destiny given by God. I am not in favor of the leftist politics of Jesse Jackson, but I certainly applaud his early efforts at Operation PUSH to strike the deep chord inside ghetto teenagers that says, "I am somebody."

You are somebody special. You are a unique creation of God. You are not here by accident. God has a plan for you.

The clearest statement of this truth that I know of was spoken by God Himself to the prophet Jeremiah some six hundred years before the birth of Christ. "Before I formed you in the womb, I knew you."[6]

Clearly and unmistakably, God is saying that life begins, not at physical conception but with a concept in the mind of God Himself. A special concept of a unique being made in His image—you!

Then God says that the process of formation of every human life, from the time the egg in the woman is fertilized by the seed of the man to the time a little baby is born into the world, is personally supervised by God Himself. He says, "Before I formed you in the womb."[7] Think of it—invisibly, silently, powerfully the hands of God were shaping your being deep inside your mother's womb. You are special. There is no one else in the world who is *you*.

"Before you were born," Jeremiah continues, "I sanctified you and ordained you to be a prophet to the nations."[8]

The call of God in your life—His plan for you—begins in the womb. It does not come at marriage, after graduation, or at age thirty. The perception of His call and plan may gradually develop during your life. But know this, the answer to the question "Why am I here?" was bound up in the same bundle of life that was you from the very beginning of your existence.

Government's Role

The role of government in light of God's plan is simple. Government must insure peace and freedom so that each of its citizens may freely work out on earth the special plan of God. Restraint should come only to prevent one citizen from hindering another citizen from enjoying "life, liberty, and the pursuit of happiness."

Communism is failing around the world for one simple reason. When a central government substitutes its collective plan for the citizens in place of God's individual plan for them, the result is frustration, inefficiency, lower productivity, repression, violence, tyranny, and collapse. That is why we must resist with all our might those coercive utopians who seize control of government proclaiming that they have a better plan for our lives than we do.

In the presidential campaign my major theme, repeated over and over again, was a warning that unless America returned to faith in God and individual self-reliance she was doomed. The reason is simple. Government money is like a narcotic. Dulling the senses.

Robbing the user of power over his own destiny. Ultimately leaving him a helpless slave.

With over 50 percent of the American people already receiving a sizeable dose of the federal financial narcotic and with politicians always willing to buy votes with more, absent a major spiritual revival, the long-range prognosis for our nation may not be good.

The issue for you and me, then, is not whether God has a plan for us. We believe He does. What we may not know in advance is the total plan—the big picture—because some of us aren't wise enough or mature enough to be able to handle it all.

So sometimes it looks like a jumble of disconnected threads. They seemingly don't make sense. In a BBC drama in 1941–42, "The Man Born To Be King," Dorothy Sayers places Lazarus in a gathering of men and women after he had been raised from the dead.[9] The captivating dialogue goes like this:

> LAZARUS (*as he speaks, the conversation dies away into an inquisitive silence*): *This* life is like weaving at the back of the loom. All you see is the crossing of the threads. In *that* life you go round to the front and see the wonder of the pattern.
>
> THIRD WOMAN: What sort of pattern is it?
>
> LAZARUS: Beautiful and terrible. And—how can I tell you?—it is *familiar*. You have known it from all eternity. For He that made it is the form of all things, Himself both the weaver and the loom.
>
> THIRD WOMAN: I see. (*She doesn't*) But what I want to know . . .
>
> SECOND MAN: That'll do, my dear. You are talking too much.

God's plan—His tapestry—is so grand, so huge, so awesome that we in our finite states can't fully see and comprehend it. And, according to Sayers, we see only the back at this time. We're apt to walk up to that loom and start trying to tidy up the threads and strings and to rearrange the colors to suit our limited tastes. We could be messing up the master design.

As Miss Sayers noted, while we can't really see and comprehend the master tapestry that God is executing with all His creation, one day we'll see and understand it all. It will be as though we stepped to the front and backed up and behold, there it is. It will make perfect sense, and it will be beautiful.

Corrie ten Boom, the Dutch lady who suffered so severely at the hands of the Nazis, because she hid Jewish people in her home during the Second World War, had a similar artistic impression of God's plan, and she took it to a more personal level. In the introduction to her book *Tramp for the Lord*, she reflected:

Looking back across the years of my life, I can see the working of a divine pattern which is the way of God with His children. When I was in a prison camp in Holland during the war, I often prayed, "Lord, never let the enemy put me in a German concentration camp." God answered *no* to that prayer. Yet in the German camp, with all its horror, I found many prisoners who had never heard of Jesus Christ. If God had not used my sister Betsie and me to bring them to Him, they would never have heard of Him. Many died, or were killed, but many died with the Name of Jesus on their lips. They were well worth all our suffering. Faith is like radar which sees through the fog—the reality of things at a distance that the human eye cannot see.[10]

To us, the tapestry makes no sense—a twisted, knotted mass of threads, colorful, yes, yet portraying nothing but a shambles. One day, we will see it from its proper side, and we will recognize it as a glorious, harmonious tapestry by a master craftsman. It will be lovely, and the millions of twists and turns will make beautiful sense.

I can say without the slightest hesitation that the will of God in my life has always been good. Whenever there have been trials, and there have been plenty, they were invariably the prelude to something bigger, more exciting, more desirable than I could have imagined.

A Prelude to Something Bigger

Back in the early days of CBN I ran this ministry on a shoestring. The first full year's income was $8,000; the second was $20,000. We were trusting God, and unless He supplied the funds we did not spend them. Debt to me was anathema.

But in 1964, I began to get adventuresome. I was able to buy a high-powered RCA FM-radio transmitter on credit along with a vastly improved broadcast tower and antenna system. Then with the power of this 50,000-watt giant, I hired a salesman. Then a golden-voiced manager. Then a couple to produce a children's program for television. Then more publicity.

By the fall of 1965, the day of reckoning had come. We

owed $40,000, and the money was not there to pay it off. We struggled. We prayed. But we went deeper in the hole.

In desperation I went to see my multimillionaire friend and patron, Fred Beazley, with a simple request, "Please sign a note for us at the bank for $40,000."

Fred Beazley looked at my financial statements and said simply, "I have never signed anybody else's note in my life. It looks like you are bankrupt, but I think you ought to sweat it."

And sweat it I did. God had put me in a crucible. The sum involved was small by today's standard, but it seemed huge in 1965.

Why wouldn't God let us borrow the money? Why wasn't there an easy way out? I hated the pressure of unpaid bills. Why wouldn't God lift the load?

Then the November fund-raising telethon began. The results on Friday and Saturday were as disappointing as the two previous years. We were desperate. One of our staff ministers went on the air and said we were bankrupt. The emotion in his voice was obvious to the audience.

Perhaps our desperation was what God was waiting for, because a miracle began to happen. The phones in the studio exploded with pledges. As the calls poured in, the totals almost touched our telethon goal of $100,000.

But more was to come. After midnight on that Saturday night, God began to wake people out of sleep. They called in repeatedly saying, "We must pledge so we can get some sleep."

For the first time in the history of CBN a telethon was

oversubscribed. Our financial crisis was passed, but that is not the real story.

Out of that time of desperate prayer and almost jubilant giving, something took place spiritually that is still with us. You see, that telethon was called "The 700 Club Telethon." And later on that week God sent a spiritual revival to Tidewater Virginia that launched a program, "The 700 Club," which has taken the word of God's power virtually through the world.

As the Bible puts it, "Weeping may endure for a night, but joy comes in the morning."[11]

In thinking of God's plan and the sufferings that may accompany it, I am always heartened by the fact that however horrible Jesus' crucifixion was, it only lasted six hours. However horrible His visit to hell, it only lasted for three days. After the three days, it was part of God's plan to let Jesus taste the glories of resurrection power.

God's plan for you includes the incredible delights of resurrection power—power so wonderful that the apostle Peter called it, "Joy inexpressible and full of glory."[12]

An anonymous writer expressed this view of the pain and joy in our lives:

My life is but a weaving, between my God and me,
I do not choose the colors, He worketh steadily.
Ofttimes He weaveth sorrow, and I in foolish pride,
Forget He sees the upper, and I the underside.
Not till the loom is silent, and shuttles cease to fly,
Will God unroll the canvas and explain the reason why.
The dark threads are as needful in the skillful Weaver's
    hand,

As the threads of gold and silver in the pattern He has
   planned.

Anonymous

Although we will never know the full details of God's
plan until "the loom is silent," as this poet says, God does
give us some road signs along the way, to bring us into His
plan and finally home to Him. In part two of this book we
will look at the keys necessary to receiving God's direction for your life.

PART TWO

---

*Eight Keys
to Receiving
God's Direction
for Your Life*

3

Believe That God Will Guide You

Before I came down to Tidewater Virginia with my family and seventy dollars to buy a television station, I lived for a short period of time in a Presbyterian parsonage located in a black slum in Brooklyn, New York. I was a graduate from seminary, a graduate from law school, a former businessman with a large multinational corporation. I had a wife and three children.

God had called me into the ministry, but where was His place of service? I was ready to go anywhere—the jungles of South America, the jungles of Africa, or the slums of New York.

We were staying temporarily in an old brownstone in what had once been a very fine neighborhood. My friend, Dick Simmons, was the pastor of the old Classon Avenue Presbyterian Church on the corner of Classon and Monroe in what is called Bedford-Stuyvesant. The old church seated about fourteen hundred people. On a good Sunday Dick Simmons had forty or fifty in attendance.

There was crime, poverty, filth, ignorance, superstition, drugs, alcoholism, family break-up. Above all there was a desperate need in that neighborhood for the gospel of Jesus Christ.

Dede and I had three fair-skinned, blue-eyed, red-headed children. Except for one Jewish merchant and a few Puerto Ricans, we were a tiny island of white in a sea of black faces.

Next door to the parsonage was another brownstone. It was for sale. The previous tenant, a black woman, was running a black bordello there. When she missed a payment on her contract of sale, she and her girls were evicted and the house was taken away from her.

One evening when Dede and I were alone, I asked the question, "Honey, if God leads us would you be willing to buy that house next door and start a mission to these people?" I knew that she had cried herself to sleep many nights, thinking of what had been happening to her and our children there. But a profound change had taken place in her life. She looked at me and said very simply, "If this is what God wants for us, I will be with you."

The next night I wanted to pray about this matter until I had received a clear direction from God. I had been completely surrendered to whatever God wanted in my life. Now Dede, who frankly had been fighting the frightening prospects of an uncertain life of faith, had joined me.

I entered the old church after dark. One naked light bulb hung over the pulpit. I sat on the floor of the platform with my Bible in my hand. "Lord," I prayed, "show me Your will. If it is Your will for us to stay in Brooklyn and start a mission, then make it clear." I waited quietly, expectantly.

I did not have to wait very long. The voice I had known spoke to my inner man: *Jeremiah 16:2.* That was all I needed.

My hands were trembling as I leafed through the Bible
to the book of the prophet Jeremiah, the sixteenth chapter, the second verse. To this day this passage is one of the
sweetest verses in the entire Bible: "You shall not take a
wife, nor shall you have sons or daughters in this place."

I jumped to my feet, snapped off the light, ran out of
the church and into the rectory. Finally, I arrived at our
bedroom door. "Honey, we are leaving Brooklyn! I have
heard from the Lord."

You see, God was waiting for Dede and me to be in
harmony, both of us completely yielded to whatever His
will was for our lives. Once we made that commitment, He
began to reveal His plan.

We left Brooklyn on November 17, 1959. I did not return with my wife and children to that place until the day
I announced my candidacy for the presidency on October 1, 1987, on the steps of the old brownstone house on
Monroe Street, just a few houses down from the now va-
cant lot where the old Classon Avenue Presbyterian
Church once stood.

Does God Speak to Us?

During the presidential campaign, it became a matter
of some interest to the press to question me about
whether God spoke to me and how He spoke to me. Their
goal was to portray me as a wild-eyed fanatic who heard
voices.

Jesus warned His disciples not to scatter pearls before
swine, lest they "turn and tear you to pieces."[1] Swine root

for and appreciate acorns to eat, not priceless pearls, which are inedible. Feed pearls worth a fortune to a boar hog and he will be so infuriated that he will try to slash you with his tusks.

I soon learned to avoid religious language and idioms during the campaign because they only invited the slashing tusks of the press. So one day I answered a reporter's question, "Does God speak to you?" by saying, "If I had worked for IBM for thirty years, wouldn't it be expected that during that time my supervisor would communicate his directions to me?" Then I went on, "I have worked for the Lord for thirty years. Wouldn't you expect that during that period of time He would communicate His directions to me as well?"

The reporter laughed and that seemed to settle the matter.

The first key to receiving God's direction for your life is: *Believe that guidance is possible.* As the Bible puts it, "He who comes to God must believe that He is, and that He is a rewarder of those who diligently seek Him."[2] God does not give up His secrets to the casual dilettante. Only to those who diligently keep on asking, keep on seeking, keep on knocking.

Moses, a Man Who Kept On Asking

Moses is considered by Jews and Christians as one of the greatest leaders of all time.

Moses was born at a time in ancient Egypt when a cruel Pharaoh had decreed the genocide of the Jewish people living in his country. Pharaoh's method was sim-

ple. Since the ancient Egyptians did not have available today's abortion clinics, capable of destroying hundreds of
thousands of unborn children, Pharaoh decreed mass in-
fanticide against all of the male babies born to Hebrew
women. As soon as Hebrew babies cleared the birth ca-
nal, the midwives in attendance were to strangle or suffo-
cate them.

But God had a different plan for one little Hebrew boy
later named Moses. Every child in Sunday school has
learned the story. The midwife in attendance saw that
Moses was an unusually attractive child, and she determined to risk Pharaoh's wrath by saving the little fellow's
life.

It was too dangerous to leave the baby at home, so
Moses' family came up with a plan to float him in a water-
proof bassinet among the reeds at the edge of the river
where Pharaoh's daughter came each day to bathe.

She heard the baby crying, had him pulled from the
water, then adopted him as her own son. Pharaoh's
daughter even hired his own mother as a wet nurse for
him.

What irony to think that God Almighty had caused the
very Hebrew who one day would destroy Pharaoh's
power to become Pharaoh's adoptive grandson!

God's plan to rescue His people would require over
eighty years to perform. He chose one little baby and
slowly, gently prepared him through a series of seemingly natural circumstances, coincidences, fortuitous
moves to lead a nation out of captivity. During the first
forty years of his life, Moses became "learned in all the
wisdom of the Egyptians."[3] He learned statecraft, law, mil-

itary tactics, science, mathematics, and astronomy. It is not unreasonable to believe that he could have ascended to the throne of Egypt as successor to Pharaoh.

But God's plan for Moses did not include the leadership of Egypt. God planned for the creation of a totally new nation destined by God to bring forth to the entire world a pure book, The Holy Bible, not one contaminated by the superstition of Egyptian sorcery and magic, and to arrange a setting out of which would come, some fourteen hundred years later, the Savior of all mankind.

So to fulfill God's plan, Moses' rapid career advancement in Egypt had to be cut short. One day he had everything that the world counts as success—fame, power, money, servants, luxury, a seemingly unlimited future. Then, in a burst of passion, he stabbed to death an Egyptian who was oppressing a Hebrew. The next day Moses was a fugitive from justice.

But in God's plan, Moses was not finished. He was just beginning.

He became a shepherd in the vast Sinai desert. He learned sorrow. He learned solitude. He developed a vast reservoir of strength within himself. His body became rock hard. He learned to walk for days in the blistering desert sun. He learned to subsist on goat's milk, cheese, and the flat bread we know as pita.

For forty years he had learned to be a king. For the next forty years he learned to be a shepherd.

Until he reached eighty years of age, Moses' knowledge of God's plan for his life was much like that of millions of people in the world today. They believe in God, but they also believe that the things that happen in their lives are the result of wise planning, coincidence, or just plain luck. They have been taught that people do not have a "pipeline" to God, so they, like Moses, do not consciously look for a master plan. They try to make things happen or they let them happen (we have fancy names, *proactive* or *reactive*, to describe these attitudes), but always these people live and think on a human, not a divine, plane.

Yet in Moses' life and in our lives there is the watchful hand of God—usually unseen and unrecognized. The apostle Paul tells us that, "We know that all that happens to us is working for our good if we love God and are fitting into his plans."[4]

People have said to me, "You missed God's will when you ran for the presidency." Not so. Why not? Because God will take all the events in the lives of those who love Him—even their mistakes, if this was a mistake—and shape them together for good.

It is debatable whether Moses' killing of an Egyptian was an act of justice or a lawless act of rage. Whichever it was, we could say, "Moses missed God's plan when he killed the Egyptian." I disagree. The killing of the Egyptian was shaped by God as an integral part of God's ultimate plan for Moses and for the Hebrew people.

If you love God, don't waste time worrying over the "if-onlys" of your life: "If only I had bought the ranch in Orange County in 1950"; "If only I had gotten into the market in '82"; "If only I had gone to law school"; "If only I had married my real sweetheart."

That's not the way it works in the real world. Silently,

invisibly, supernaturally, God is taking the actions of those who love Him—even Adam's original sin—and is shaping them into His plan. After all, since God knows the end from the beginning, He already has taken into account everything you will do in your life—good or bad.

Enemies Can Play a Part in God's Plan

The enemies of God are part of His plan as well. Like Ahab the king of Israel, they cannot interfere with God's will. Certainly Ahab tried. God warned Ahab that he would die in an upcoming battle with the Syrians. Ahab determined to frustrate God's plan. First, he put armor on his body, which covered his entire chest; then he put on additional armor that covered his abdominal area. The only exposed area was a place about the size of a silver dollar at his navel where the armor plates met.

Next, Ahab put off his splendid robes and put on the garments of a common soldier. To finish the preparation, Ahab encouraged his ally, King Jehoshaphat, to wear his full regalia so that he, not Ahab, would become a target for the Syrian troops.

But in one of those "coincidences" of history, we learn that the Syrian king had ordered his cavalry only to fight against Ahab of Israel.

When the battle got underway, the Syrian charioteers were, at first, fooled by Ahab's deception and they raced for King Jehoshaphat. Soon they learned that they were pursuing the wrong king.

As the troops milled about, one Syrian archer "drew a

bow at random."⁵ In modern slang we might say, "He fired off a round in the air for kicks." That unaimed Syrian arrow flew into the air, and then, as if guided by an unseen hand, sped straight at the chink in King Ahab's armor: the place at his navel the size of a silver dollar. The arrow plunged into his body and mortally wounded him.⁶

Was the Syrian archer aware that he was part of God's plan? Of course not.

Each one of us who sincerely loves God can rest secure in the consciousness that God's plan will be worked out for us. Above us is the all-seeing eye of a watchful, heavenly Father. Underneath us are His everlasting arms. He even "gives His beloved sleep."⁷

Yet many of us are in too much of a hurry to wait for God's direction, just as our forefathers in the Bible. We, like Nicodemus, want quick answers without any long-term changes in life-style.

Seeing the Pattern

Late one night in Jerusalem when most of the city was asleep, there was a light tapping on the door of the room where Jesus was staying. When Jesus opened the door, He found a prominent, wealthy member of the Israeli parliament (the Sanhedrin), whose name was Nicodemus, standing in the shadows. He had come at night because he did not wish to jeopardize his political career by being seen in the company of this radical preacher from Galilee.

Nicodemus wasted no time on small talk. "Rabbi," he said, "we know that You are a teacher come from God."⁸ In other words, "I want you to tell me how to find God's will and God's power for my life."

Jesus shot back, "Unless one is born again, he cannot see the kingdom of God. . . . unless one is born of water and the Spirit, he cannot enter the kingdom of God."[9]

You see, Nicodemus, like so many of us today, wanted a quick fix. People want to find a holy man, an Indian Guru, a priest, a rabbi, an evangelist, or a New Age psychic to give them a glimpse into the mystery of the unknown. They want a teaching or a ritual or a magic crystal or a seance that will let them know with certainty that their lives are headed in the right direction. They want to touch the supernatural, but they want magic, not a new life. They are like former Beatle George Harrison, who sings to Hari Krishna in his song "My Sweet Lord": "I want to see you, Lord. I want to know you, Lord."[10]

God's plan is not magic. His kingdom is available to everyone, but it may be seen and entered only by those who have been "born again."

Quite simply, God's kingdom power and the revelation of His will can only come to those who have repented from their sins, have received God's offer of forgiveness through the sacrificial death of Jesus Christ, and have confessed Jesus Christ as Lord of every aspect of their lives. Then, and only then, will the Holy Spirit of God come upon them, transforming their eyes and opening their ears so they can truly see and hear about the king-dom of God and God's miraculous plan for every human being.

The apostle Paul described the experience to the Church at Corinth when he wrote,

Eye has not seen, nor ear heard,
Nor have entered into the heart of man
The things which God has prepared
For those who love Him,
But God has revealed them to us through His Spirit.[11]

It is God's will that born-again people, who have been baptized by His glorious Spirit, will have continuous guidance.

David spoke of it when he wrote, "Who is the man who fears the LORD? Him shall He teach in the way He chooses."[12]

Jesus Christ said, "The Father has not left me alone, for I always do those things that please Him."[13]

Without question it is God's will for you and me to know God's plan for our life, to hear His voice, and to be led by His Spirit continually. It is not God's intention for those who know Him to grope about in the darkness without any direction for their lives.

If God had told Moses to free the Hebrew slaves before Moses spent those forty years in the wilderness, he would probably have tried to raise an army to accomplish the release of the Hebrew people from slavery in Egypt. There would have been violence, bloodshed, and death. If the effort had succeeded, Moses would have received the credit for it. Most likely such an uprising would have been crushed. In either case God would not have been glorified. There would have been no plagues on Egypt. No Passover. No parting of the Red Sea. No manna or quail in the wilderness. No pillar of cloud or pillar of fire.

God had a plan, but His plan called for a man who was

so humble and yielded to God that He would attempt God's direction to rescue an entire nation, armed only with God's mandate and a long staff.

Daily, God spoke to Moses, and Moses brought forth God's miracles, God's Passover, God's parting of the Red Sea, and God's laws for the nation of Israel.

Not only did Moses hear God's voice, Moses ascended to the top of Mount Sinai and saw the glory of God. While he was there for forty days and forty nights, God gave him two patterns. One was the pattern for the civil government of the nation; the other was the pattern for the tabernacle, the center of worship for the nation.

Later, God said to Moses, "Raise up the tabernacle according to its pattern which you were shown on the mountain."[14]

You see all that is in the universe began with a concept in the mind of God. He has a pattern for nature, a pattern for government, a pattern for family life, a pattern for business, a pattern for agriculture, a pattern for labor relations, a pattern for education, and, of course, a pattern for His church. Then, He has a pattern for the life of each human being, and the relationship of all human beings to one another and to the nations. Finally, He has a pattern to end this age and bring about a new heaven and new earth where His love, His peace, and His joy will reign supreme.

God said to Moses, "Make the tabernacle after the pattern I showed you on the mountain."

He says to each one of us, "To be happy and to be successful, design your life and the institutions you touch according to the pattern that I will show you on your mountain top with me." Your task is to find the pattern made for you in heaven, then live it out on earth.

I believe that this, at least in part, is what Jesus meant when He taught us to pray to the Father, "Your will be done on earth as it is in heaven."[15]

4

Surrender to His Will for You

The stately Homestead Hotel in Hot Springs, Virginia, spreads a buffet every day at noon time of an overwhelming array of delicacies. Cold shrimp salad, lobster salad, artichoke hearts, various types of cold fish and cold cuts, an awesome array of pickles, then hot fish, game, and leg of lamb, corn pudding, hot vegetables, and a dessert table with premium ice cream, various sundaes, tarts, eclairs, cakes, and much, much more.

No one human could try it all. So the guests sample a bit of this and a little bit of that and bypass the rest.

The plan of God for your life is *not* like this smorgasbord where you can walk around the table, choose what you like, and leave the rest. God has made no provision for those who will skip the sour pickles and take the sweets. The courses in God's plan come at you one at a time. Rarely, if ever, will you get a glimpse of the entire menu. If you or I refuse the bitter cup, we may not have a chance to taste the sweet one.

Jesus Christ put it this way, "If anyone wants to do His will he shall know concerning the doctrine."[1] In other words, revelation follows surrender and obedience, not the other way around. The second key to receiving God's direction for your life is: *Be willing to surrender to His will for you.*

You might ask, "But doesn't that sound like buying 'a pig in a poke'?" Not really. The reason is simple. God commended His love toward us that while we were His enemies—sinners—Christ died for us. He has no further need to prove His love to us. It is forever settled.

When we receive Jesus Christ as our Savior, we have accepted God's gift of unconditional love. The apostle Paul spoke of our salvation by the unmerited favor or grace of God, then he said we have been "created in Christ Jesus for good works, which God prepared beforehand that we should walk in them."[2] The challenge for you and me, having already surrendered to the eternal plan of God for our salvation, is to surrender now to the temporal plan of good works, which God has laid out for us in this life.

But remember the priorities. Jesus' disciples went out on a preaching mission, then returned wild-eyed in amazement at the demonstration of His power. "Lord," they said, "even the demons are subject to us in Your name."[3]

Jesus sensed that youthful exuberance we all have when we experience a miracle taking place in our lives. Then very gently He reestablished to them what was really important. "Do not rejoice in this, that the spirits are subject to you," He said, "but rather rejoice because your names are written in heaven."[4]

Surrender the Details to God

If you can trust God to take your dead body and resurrect it brand new—if you can trust God to cause your immortal spirit to fly through space to another world—

why is it so hard to trust God for this week's house payment and grocery money?

Revelation Follows Surrender

Dede and I learned that in Brooklyn when Dede surrendered to the will of God and then He immediately revealed the next step. We were to leave Brooklyn, take our family and our limited possessions in a small U-Haul trailer, and travel to Portsmouth, Virginia, where, with seventy dollars and no television experience, I was to buy a television station for His glory.

As we obeyed that step, God revealed the next—a network of stations. Then the next—overseas stations. Then a satellite cable television network. Then a major relief agency. Then a graduate university. Then a television station in Israel. Then an organization to alert Christians to the erosion of their freedoms. And, yes, a run for the presidency of the United States to call a nation back to its moral roots.

All I did was obey. As God led me, I tried to carry out His will. As I obeyed one step faithfully, He would show me another step in His plan.

Revelation Follows Obedience

But always remember, *what you are is more important than what you do*. Many religious people have been snared by the tyranny of results. Ministers think because they draw big crowds, see miracles, win thousands to Jesus Christ, and raise the money to pay for it all that they are in the center of God's plan. Businessmen also equate financial gain with godliness.

Shouldn't it be more important that they exchange pride for a meek spirit? That they love their brothers? That they evidence gentleness and self-control and faith? That they love their wives or husbands and order their households well?

Jesus warned us that in the last days many would come to Him and declare that they had cast out demons and done mighty works in His name. He rebuked them saying, "I never knew you; depart from Me, you who practice lawlessness."[5] He promised to receive everyone "who does the will of My Father in heaven."[6]

God's standard of judgment is based on obedience and knowledge. The more we know, the more responsibility we carry. Jesus said it this way, "That servant who knew his master's will, and did not prepare himself or do according to his will shall be beaten with many stripes. . . . He who did not know, yet committed things worthy of stripes, will be beaten with few."[7]

The apostle James warned the people of his day to be very careful about being teachers because those who set themselves in authority to teach others would be held to a much higher standard.[8]

Lucifer, the highest of the created beings, will one day be confined in a horrible lake of fire. His punishment is the most harsh because his privilege was the very highest. He was permitted to learn the secrets of the Godhead, to know firsthand the fullness of the glory of God.

When he revolted against God, he did so with absolute knowledge and absolute privilege. Therefore, for Lucifer (now called Satan, the adversary) there can be no forgiveness and no repentance.

Think what would happen if God lifted you to heaven and then laid out a complete blueprint for your life for you. What if you saw sights a human being should not see and heard voices that humans should not hear, and then you returned to earth and rebelled against the revelation that you received? You would have no excuse and no real chance to repent. Your only future would be to spend eternity alone with Satan in hell.

God loves us too much to let that happen. That is why He makes sure of our dedication to His plan before He begins to reveal parts of it to us. Jesus showed Himself to the apostle Paul and spoke to him.

Paul was ready for the revelation. Later, he proudly told King Agrippa, "Therefore, I was not disobedient to the heavenly vision."⁹ Paul obeyed. Unfortunately most people today reject any form of obedience.

Have No Mind of Your Own

George Muller of Bristol, England, is one of the most unusual men of Christian history. He established an orphange in Victorian England where he regularly fed, clothed, and housed two thousand orphans. Yet George Muller never admitted a need, never sent out a fundraising letter, never communicated a desire for material help to any living human being.

All the money and guidance Muller needed to perform his remarkable ministry came by the grace of God in answer to prayer. When he was asked the secret of his remarkable access to God in prayer and divine guidance, Muller replied, "Have no mind of your own in the matter."

What did he mean by this? Certainly not that we should be mindless robots. He obviously did not mean that we should go contrary to the Bible itself and "forsake wisdom."[10] Muller meant that when he sought God's leading he did not come with a preconceived notion of what he wanted to have accomplished.

So many people map out their own plans and then bring these plans to God to get His stamp of approval. They want to buy a house, and they ask God to lead them to buy it. They want to start a career, and they ask God to lead them into it. They want to marry a mate, and they ask God to lead them into the marriage. They want a divorce, and they ask God to lead them out of their marriage.

Their glib reply to any questions about their conduct is, "The Lord told me to do this" or "I don't feel led to do that." What they actually are saying is that they are going to do what they please and use God to justify their actions.

To receive pure guidance from the Lord you need to come to God without a hidden agenda. At the center of your being there needs to be one resolve—"Not my will but Your will be done." Since we are human beings with sinful desires and passions, we often need a protracted period of prayer to bring our desires into conformity with His. (It took Moses forty years on the "back of the desert"[11] to be ready to receive God's plan.)

Even Jesus Christ, the sinless Son of God, had to pray

three times in the Garden of Gethsemane, "Thy will be done," as He faced the cross and the agony of separation from the Father and the horror of drinking the filthy cup of hell, brimming with every bestial, cruel sin that every human being on earth had ever committed. In Gethsemane, known as the "olive press," He sweat blood in agony as His human will was brought into absolute surrender to the will of the Father.

Not My Will But . . .

In 1984, my life was near perfect. The ministry of CBN was hitting undreamed-of heights. The audience on our "700 Club" television program was the largest of any religious program in America, reaching 29 million people each month. Tens of thousands were meeting Jesus Christ. There were many miracles of healing. Our cable network had seen its audience go up 300 percent the previous year. Our Operation Blessing relief effort alone was facilitating close to $50 million a year in community support for relief to the poor. CBN University was flourishing, our overseas ministry was flourishing, and our new television station on the border of Lebanon was a fulfillment of a dream. Our prime time special, "Don't Ask ME; Ask God" was the most watched religious special in history. Dede and I had moved into a lovely residence on the CBN campus; three of my children and two little grandchildren were living in the area. My book *The Secret Kingdom* was a national best seller. I had so much income that I was able to give back all of my CBN salary and more. I even had some horses to enjoy. Chuck Colson once commented, "Pat, you've got it made."

Then that still voice I had known so well: *You will not want to do it, but I want you to be president of the United States.*

I asked for confirmation from Scripture. It came repeatedly. On my knees I wrestled with God. "Father," I prayed, "in all the years I have served you I have only glorified You, not myself. I don't want to go into an arena where the cheers will be for me and not for You. I don't want to do it."

I prayed almost every day for three years. I literally begged God not to let me be misled. I said, "Father, I am a broadcaster and a Bible teacher. How can I function in a world of complex political issues?"

After months of prayer, I said simply with tears in my eyes, "If this is indeed Your will I will do it. I am willing to lose everything I have, but one thing I will not give up—my closeness with You." Without my saying a word about any of this to more than a couple of very close friends, people began coming to me, asking me to run for president. Some reported dreams, revelations, inner leading. Then amazingly, Dr. Cory SerVaas, the publisher of the *Saturday Evening Post*, decided to do a cover story about me in the March 1985 issue of her magazine. The topic, "What's Ahead for Pat Robertson?" Here's how this story began:

The *Post* has for some months been hearing a rustling among the grass roots in the land. It centers on an unusual man—a broadcaster, a lawyer, an economist, a theologian, a businessman—named Pat Robertson, the president of a burgeoning communications-education complex grouped around the Christian Broadcasting Network.

The rustling—gentle but persistent—usually takes the form of a question, or perhaps two questions run together. They go something like this: "What is Pat Robertson going to do next? Do you think he'll one day run for president?" The *Post* found that, often, the questions pop up in discussions about successors to Ronald Reagan. Furthermore, the *Post* found that the questioners are serious.[12]

After the *Post* article, outside interest literally exploded.

But I continued in prayer. Day after day the same thing—"Father, I want only Your will. Don't let me be misled." But this was just the beginning. There were many more difficult signs that I asked from the Lord before I could say that a run for the presidency was God's plan for me.

The Hurricane

In the fall of each year at CBN we celebrate the biblical ceremony of Rosh Hashana, the Jewish New Year, and we continue special programs through what is called the Feast of Tabernacles, or Succoth.

The fall of 1985 was no exception. I was on the television set when our producer, Terry Heaton, came over and whispered in my ear, "There's a big hurricane in the Atlantic and it's heading our way."

This was one piece of news I absolutely did not need.

Since the early days of CBN, we had widely publicized the fact that on two separate occasions killer hurricanes had been diverted from our area in response to prayer. In fact, though our part of the Atlantic Coast had once been known as "Hurricane Alley," we had not had a hurricane hit the region in over twenty years. These miracles were clearly recorded in my two books, *The Secret Kingdom* and *Beyond Reason.*

In 1985, I was two people. One believed and taught the miracle power of God as a religious broadcaster, pastor, and teacher. The other was being scrutinized by the secular public as a potential political leader. If I prayed the way I knew how to pray, the secular world would say I was a religious fanatic. If I didn't pray as was needed, the storm would hit us and the faith of millions would be damaged.

I knew the "political" risk, but I really had no choice. I went on television and was joined in prayer by thousands of believers as we commanded the hurricane in the name of Jesus Christ to move out into the Atlantic. A day went by. The hurricane picked up intensity and continued straight for the coast of Virginia. I called a staff meeting, and together we prayed with all the intensity at our command. My producer taped the prayer meeting and ran it across America on the special "700 Club" program of the next day. (This was the video that greeted me when I appeared on the NBC Show "Meet the Press" later that year.)

While I was praying alone after our prayer meeting, the Lord assured me that the hurricane would not hit our area. Still, all that day the monster storm bore down on us. A feeling of gloom descended on me. My prayers were not being answered, and now it seemed that what I had long known as God's still small voice was misleading me. The faith of our staff, the faith of my audience, and my own future was on the line. I realized all too well that if the supernatural presence of God that I had known for almost thirty years had left me, I would be absolutely helpless in the alien arena of politics.

My son, his family, and some of my daughter's friends who lived near the ocean decided to spend the night at our house for safety's sake. Soon our home took on the festive nature of a slumber party. As I watched everyone laughing and playing games, a feeling of deep melancholy began to grip me. The news at nine gave me no comfort. The storm was 105 miles south of Norfolk and was due to hit land shortly after midnight.

At 9:15 I knelt on the floor of my small dressing room and poured my heart out to the Lord. "Father," I said, "if I can't move a storm, how can I move a nation? Father, I am laying a fleece out before You. If this storm hits our area, I am out of the presidential race completely."

Gideon's Fleece

This type of prayer for confirmation of God's will began with Gideon, a young farmer in ancient Israel. One day he received a strange visitor who brought him an even stranger greeting, "The LORD is with you, you mighty man of valor!"[13] The farmer was not a soldier nor a politician. In his eyes, he certainly wasn't a "mighty man of valor." He was a simple man of the people, eking a living from the rocky soil of the land.

Yet here was an angel sent by God to deliver a plan to Gideon. God had chosen Gideon to break the stronghold that an alien people, the Midianites, held on the nation of Israel. Even though Gideon had heard the message and seen the messenger face-to-face, he wanted further proof before he launched a military action that could cost his life.

So Gideon designed a simple plan. He took a sheep-skin—called a fleece—and left it outside. Then he asked God to confirm His plan for him by a sign. If the fleece was wet with dew and the ground was dry, he would know. The next morning the fleece was so soaked that he could wring containers of water from it.

But Gideon was still reluctant. God's plan for him was so outrageous that he asked for a second sign. This time a reverse of the first. He placed the fleece outside for a night and asked that the fleece be dry and the ground wet. Lo and behold, the next morning dew was on the ground, but the fleece was dry as a bone.

These signs were all the confirmation Gideon needed. He plunged into action. With an army of only three hundred men and with God's strategic plan and miraculous intervention, Gideon routed the vastly superior Midianite army and drove them from his country.[14]

When some Christian people today ask for an outward sign from God to confirm a more subjective inner leading, they use the term, "I put out a fleece."

In my opinion a confirming sign for every decision should be unnecessary for mature Christians. It certainly would seem presumptuous to ask the God of the universe to provide a sign to authenticate some trivial change of plans. But Gideon was being asked to leave his occupation and start a war between two nations. I, too, was making a decision that would affect many people. I knew that our God is gracious and would confirm His word to me or you when such confirmation was truly necessary.

The basic rule is this: Big decisions require big guidance. God would not expect anyone to embark on a major change in his or her life on the strength of some inner voice. Like the call of Gideon of old or my call in 1984, God will give massive confirmation to make His plan certain.

God's Answer to My Fleece

When I finished praying the words, "If this storm hits our area, I am out of the presidential race completely," a feeling of almost indescribable relief came over me. The burden was gone. I was out of politics! Tomorrow I would do a "Sherman": "If nominated I will not run. If elected, I will not serve." I fell asleep almost as soon as my head touched the pillow.

At 4:00 A.M. I woke up and looked out the window. Except for a strong wind everything looked normal. I went downstairs, stepping carefully over girls in sleeping bags on the way through the front hall to the den. I switched on the weather channel and heard the news. Just before the massive hurricane hit land, the storm suddenly veered east and was now out to sea forty-five miles northeast of Norfolk.

God had answered our prayers. Our region had been

spared, but I was back in the presidential race. Only now I had been labeled the nut who thinks he can pray away hurricanes.

God's Direction for CBN

God has an awesome array of ways by which He can communicate His will to us: the Bible, His inner voice, His peace in our hearts, the advice of others, confirming circumstances, visions, dreams, angelic visitors, and specific, extraordinary signs. Such a sign concerned the nation of Israel, and I received one in 1981.

On June 5, 1967, we began a new studio building for CBN. On that same day, the Six Day War broke out between Israel and her neighbors. I had been aware for years of the role of Israel in prophecy and attached no small significance to these concurrent events.

The next year, I made my first trip to Israel for the purpose of exploring broadcast opportunities there. I traveled in the spring, just prior to Passover when there was a full moon. I left London on a British European Airways jet and was traveling about 9:00 P.M. just south of the Turkish coast when God spoke to me: *You are entering Israel, the land of the Bible. You made mistakes in Portsmouth. You made mistakes in New York. You made mistakes in South America. You are not to make any mistakes here.*

I was awestruck at what I had just heard. Then I realized that events in Israel were planned by God to fulfill biblical prophecy. The wrong broadcast operations in Israel could change prophecy—and God would never permit that to happen. No mistakes meant just that! *No mistakes!*

I tried for the next ten years to obtain permission to broadcast into or out of Israel. Nothing happened.

Then in 1978 my friend George Otis of High Adventure Ministries informed me that he had received permission from Major Haddad, the Lebanese military commander in Southern Lebanon, to operate a radio station just north of the Israeli border near Metulla.

I knew this was an unusual opportunity for ministry, and after prayer I made a missionary gift of a hundred thousand dollars from CBN to High Adventure Ministries to build the station.

The next move was unexpected and spectacular. In November of 1981, George Otis asked to have lunch with me, my wife, Dede, and our CBN board members Bob Slosser and Tucker Yates. Over lunch at the Ramada Inn in Virginia Beach, George opened his "surprise." It seemed that he had more recently built a television station on Channel 12 in Southern Lebanon. He did not have the funds to operate it properly, and he wanted to give it to CBN. He said very earnestly, "I am not going to stand in the way of the coming of Jesus Christ by holding on to this station."

My first inclination was to grasp his hand and say, "It's a deal." But I remembered the Lord's warning from 1968. "No mistakes." I also remembered that the station was located in a war zone, and could be blown up at any time. Prudence demanded a clear word from the Lord—very big guidance! So I said, "George, it's a wonderful offer. Let us pray about it and we will get back to you."

The next morning, Thursday, in my devotional time, I picked up my Bible. It opened to the story of Gideon and the fleece. As I thought about this bit of biblical history for a few minutes I realized that God wanted to give me a confirming sign on the Lebanon station, just like the sign that he had given Gideon. So I said, "Lord, I believe that You want me to ask for a 'fleece.'" But what kind of fleece could I ask for? After a few minutes, a thought came to me. "If something of gold comes to CBN or me in the next several days," I prayed, "I will take it as a sign that you want us to take over the station in Lebanon from George Otis."

Then I waited. Thursday no gold. Friday no gold. Saturday no gold. Then on Sunday, I said to Dede, "We have to pray about that Lebanon station. It's too important to wait much longer."

So we sat at our dining room table, and we asked God to speak to our minds those passages in His Word that would give us direction in this crucial matter. The Lord directed me to a brief passage in John's gospel, describing an instance when Jesus opened the eyes of the blind.

I turned to Dede and asked what God had showed her. She seemed perplexed. "He gave me Isaiah 29, and I can't make any sense out of it." She handed me her Bible and I read the words of the prophet Isaiah:

Is it not yet a very little while
Till Lebanon shall be a fruitful field,

And the fruitful field shall be esteemed as a forest?
In that day the deaf shall hear the words of the book,
And the eyes of the blind shall see . . . .[15]

God had given Dede the answer. This was a Messianic scripture that was tied to a spiritual awakening in Lebanon. "Do you see what God has shown us?" I almost shouted. "Revival and awakening are to come out of Lebanon where the TV station is located. Jesus is going to teach the Bible to the spiritually deaf and He is going to open the eyes of those who are spiritually blind."

(Only later did I learn that God had used this very biblical passage as His key inspiration to George Otis to go forward and build the High Adventure radio station in southern Lebanon.)

I wanted that station so badly that I felt I had all the guidance I needed. But I had asked for a "fleece" of gold, and I could not move without it.

On Monday evening Dede and I were going to have dinner after work at a restaurant in Norfolk. On her way to the studio to meet me, she stopped by our private mailbox, a small box for magazine subscriptions, bank statements, and bills, to get the day's mail. Hardly anyone else knew about it.

After we were seated for dinner, I glanced through the letters and found one from my dear friend Frank Foglio of San Diego, California. As I opened the letter and glanced at its contents, my heart seemed to stick in my throat. Inside that letter was a photograph of four, priceless, 24-karat gold medallions struck from a mold crafted by Pablo Picasso.

Only six of these medallions existed in the world, and Frank had four of them. He wanted to make one or two of them available to CBN.

Here was my gold "fleece" from the Lord. Not a piece of 14-karat jewelry, or even a one-ounce Krugerand, but an artistic rarity. A piece which is now in CBN's possession and worth an estimated fifty to one hundred thousand dollars.

I never found out how Frank learned the number of my private post office box. But he did tell me that he had felt a strong urging of the Lord to send the information to me quickly. In fact, he had sent two letters. The first unknown to him was lost, but because he "forgot" to include the pictures of the coins, he sent a second letter which did get through—five days after I had asked God for a confirming sign. It seems that God even has back-up protection against failures in the United States Postal Service!

On April 10, 1982, in a fulfillment of the desire of my heart, CBN took over what we now call Middle East Television. Since that time it has developed a huge audience in Lebanon, Jordan, Israel, and Syria. Some reports indicate that it may be the most popular station in the area. The spiritual results among Jews and Arabs are amazing. Yet we are just beginning to see what will take place when the war in Lebanon comes to an end and Lebanon becomes the "fruitful field" that the Bible promises.

Can we with our finite minds even begin to fathom the incredible complexity of God's plan in just one life? The intertwining of events, the interplay of lives, the preparation of circumstances, the preparation of the life of the one involved, and the slow, painstaking, revelation of little pieces of the plan until everything is in place.

We, like the apostle Paul, step back in awe, and exclaim:
    Oh, the depth of the riches both of the wisdom and
        knowledge of God!
    How unsearchable are His judgments and His ways
        past finding out!
    For of Him and through Him and to Him are all
        things.[16]

5

Practice God's Will Every Day

I t was a warm, spring Friday in 1968. After "The 700 Club" broadcast, I was driving along a main street, not far from our studios in Portsmouth, and was struck with the idea that I should go to see my friend and benefactor, Fred Beazley. It was just an idea, maybe an urging.

I had been in the ministry for about fifteen years and had practiced walking with the Lord. I had worked at being aware of His presence and of thinking about Him no matter what I was doing. But the idea of going to see Fred, a busy man who had made a nice, comfortable home available to me and had been a good friend and counselor in other ways, didn't seem to fit.

This is silly, I thought. *I don't need to go see him. He has a lot of other things on his mind, and I am just too busy.*

The following Monday, it was announced that Fred had given the beautiful property that I had lived on for four years to the state community college system. And I was going to be a tenant. Subsequently, the state sold a part of the property to a sewage treatment plant. After 1981 my continued living there became intolerable.

That Monday I was immediately aware that I had missed God's guidance. *That was stupid,* I thought. *If I'd gone to see him, the chances are he would have given the house I was living in to CBN.* It was on the edge of one thousand acres and probably would have made little financial difference to him whether it had been included in his gift to the state or not.

The point was clear. I had received a signal, but I had ignored it. God had prepared a pleasant gift for me if only I had heeded the prompting of the Spirit. But I mistook the prompting of the Holy Spirit for an impulse of my own mind.

Yes, that was a good lesson about receiving God's guidance. It called for being conscious and sensitive, ready for whatever the Lord had for me.

This sensitivity and consciousness is part of the principle I wrote about in *The Secret Kingdom.* It's the law of use and is as imperative and important as the law of gravity. We ignore it at our peril.

"To everyone who has," Jesus said, "more will be given, and he will have abundance; but from him who does not have, even what he has will be taken away."[1]

The natural man recoils and says, "But that's harsh. He who already has doesn't need more." But that's not the way the world was set up. God gives gifts to everyone, and He intends for people to use them. That use creates more, and the additional gift is used to create even more, and so on. The third key to receiving God's direction for your life is: *Practice God's will every day.*

It's like exercise. If I faithfully exercise my left arm daily, using weights or some consistent regimen, my left arm will become well-muscled and strong. But if I tape my left arm to my side, not using it for several weeks, the muscles will atrophy and become useless. What I had been given will have been taken away—all through violation of the law of use.

Use: The Way of the Professional

In the 1988 general election, Vice President George Bush started behind Governor Michael Dukakis in the polls, moved even with him after the second day of the Republican Convention, and finished the week nine points ahead.

From that point on Dukakis never had a chance. George Bush flew into Boston and pointed out the pollution in Boston harbor—Dukakis's backyard. Then Bush received the endorsement of uniformed police officers in the capital of Dukakis's own state. The Bush campaign contrasted this picture with a photograph of Dukakis wearing a ridiculous-looking helmet, driving an army tank.

When Dukakis was reciting his mantra, "Good jobs for good pay," the administration was flooding the country with news that unemployment had hit a fourteen-year low, and during the past eight years 17 million new jobs had been created.

While the Dukakis staff members were squabbling among themselves, the Bush campaign, like a well-oiled machine, was launching dozens of surrogate speakers around the country, all of them on the attack, all pointing out the theme of the week, showing another Dukakis weakness.

While Dukakis searched for a theme to gain attention,

the Bush campaign never let up on the themes that played best with Reagan Democrats according to sophisticated market research: the furlough release of Willie Horton and Dukakis's refusal to force Massachusetts teachers to recite the Pledge of Allegiance to the American flag.

While Dukakis was dancing away from the word *liberal,* the Bush campaigners had their man in downstate Illinois with country singers Loretta Lynn and Crystal Gayle talking about God and country and family values.

These things did not happen by chance. Neither Michael Dukakis nor any of his staff had ever run a presidential campaign before. George Bush had run as a vice-presidential contender in two successful national elections. He had run for president in three primary cycles. His campaign chairmen had successful presidential campaigns under their belts, plus gubernatorial and senatorial races. They marshalled their money and staff, planned their advertisements, magnified their strengths, and exploited their opponent's weaknesses. If George Bush made a mistake, his managers explained it away without a ripple of damage. The candidate and the managers who have been around the track a couple of times have an enormous advantage in a three-month campaign over enthusiastic novices who have never been there before.

In fact, it is a rare field of human endeavor where the novice has an advantage over an experienced professional. The reason is simple. God has established an order of things that mandates improvement with use. The more you study, the better you are able to comprehend. The more you exercise, the better your muscles work. The more you speak, the better you communicate.

If we use what we have, it will grow and develop. If we refuse to use what is given us, it will shrivel up and be lost. This rule applies to knowledge, muscular development, professional skills, finances, and particularly to sensitivity to God's leading.

I have told you about the pattern of guidance God has used in my life and the lives of others. You may think that this type of guidance from God is only for those engaged in religious work. Nothing could be further from the truth. All who know Jesus Christ are called saints in the New Testament. Jesus said we should call no one father or rabbi because we are all brothers and sisters, and we have only one Father, God, and one Master, Christ Himself. The Bible teaches that there is to be no distinction between male or female, slave or free, Greek or barbarian. We are all part of Christ's body.

This being the case you must realize that the same rules that govern the "professionals" also govern you, and the most important principle for us all is practice and experience.

Practicing God's Will

When I first started in the Spirit-led life in theological seminary, my friends and I would literally practice God's leading. In a service of worship, we would ask the Spirit of God to direct us. As we gave praise to the Father and the Son, we found that the Holy Spirit would begin to speak to us. In one such service God gave me the number of a hymn in the Presbyterian hymnal. At the same time another member of our group was given a psalm. To our delight we realized that the hymn was actually the psalm set to music. We were in spiritual elementary school and the Holy Spirit was our teacher.

Sometimes there would be a manifestation of the gifts of the Holy Spirit, a message in tongues with an interpretation. Sometimes a prophecy. Like a father who watches his children learn to walk and talk, our heavenly Father overlooked our mistakes and smiled at our progress.

We went out on the streets of New York seeking His leading. On one occasion my friend Harald Bredesen and I visited an all-black, high-rise tenement building in the Bronx. We did not know who to call on, so we ran our fingers down the roster of tenants until God showed us the one who not only needed His help but was willing to receive it. When my finger reached one name, I felt like someone had punched me in the stomach. "Harald," I said, "let's try this apartment."

We knocked on the door and an attractive black lady opened and looked out. "We're from a church nearby," we explained. "We'd like to visit with you for a while."

She welcomed us in.

In just a few minutes we realized that her husband was leaving her and her life was in shambles. I suggested that Jesus Christ was the answer to her problems, and invited her to pray with me. We all knelt down. I began a prayer and invited her to join me.

"Lord Jesus," I said.

"Lord Jesus," she said.

". . . I know that you died for me," I said.

". . . I know that you died for me," she repeated.

"I need your help," I said.

From then on she needed no help or coaching. A prayer literally gushed from her anguished heart. "Oh, yes, Lord Jesus. Please help me, Lord. I need You, Lord. I want to be Yours, Lord!"

That woman was gloriously led to salvation in Jesus Christ and later became a member of the First Reformed Church of Mount Vernon. As I recall, the Lord not only met her need, but the needs of her husband, her children, and her marriage.

When we knocked on her door, she had been prepared by God Himself. Her need and her openness to the Lord showed me that God's Spirit could lead me with great precision.

Unfortunately, not all of our "leadings" were on target. I remember a time when my friend, Presbyterian minister Dick Simmons felt God tell him to go to a particular address in one of the boroughs of New York. He was convinced that this was to be a place of special ministry. With some effort he located the street and followed the numbers to the place "revealed" to him: a large hole in the ground where a house had once stood.

Over the years I have learned great humility in recognizing a leading as being from God. That is why I check out my own leadings so carefully. I have absolutely no patience with these young Christians whose every phrase seems to be "God told me this" or "God led me there." Instead, I am interested in their track record. Often it is not much better than the "psychics" written up annually in

The Star and the *National Enquirer*. Each year for a laugh we at CBN track the predictions of those so-called seers. We discovered that they are wrong about 88 percent of the time. I marvel that people continue to believe such pearls as, "In 1989 Ted Kennedy will fall for the charms of Donna Rice—and announce she's going to be his wife."

For you and for me, the simple rule is "practice the presence of God." The writer of the book of Hebrews described the mature person as, "Those who by reason of use have their senses exercised to discern both good and evil."[2]

You see, in the final analysis, "good" for you is what God wants. God's will in your life, His plan for you is good. The apostle Paul called it "that good and acceptable and perfect will of God."[3]

For the entire world, the ultimate "good" is God's will. That is why we should pray with sincerity and earnestness, "Your kingdom come, Your will be done, on earth as it is in heaven."[4] Consider what the will of God on earth will mean:

- No more war, and all military schools will close, for people will no longer "study" war.
- No more greed, avarice, and covetousness. No more crime, so every person will be able to enjoy his own possessions without fear.
- Nature will be at peace. Poisonous snakes will be harmless. Wild animals will live at peace with domestic animals, and they will be so docile that "a little child can lead them."
- Sickness and disease will be eradicated, along with

alcoholism, drug abuse, and various forms of toxic pollution. People will no longer be exploited by others for greed's sake.

- Disputes between people and nations will be settled according to the just and fair principles of the law of God. As the prophet Micah put it,

"For out of Zion the Law shall go forth, . . .
Nation shall not lift up sword against nation,
Neither shall they learn war anymore.[5]

Few people believe, deep down inside, that God is a good God with a good plan of good works. Trust God's goodness. The plan of God for you is a prize beyond calculation.

The accepted way to discern that good plan is by practice and experience. As the great Bible teacher Donald Gray Barnhouse put it, "God uses oak trees, not mushrooms."

There are no shortcuts to physical maturity. The famous Olympic sprinter Ben Johnson learned to his sorrow that the quick fix provided by anabolic steroids will only lead to disgrace and in some cases death. There are no shortcuts to spiritual maturity either. The master principle calls for slow growth by trial and error, patience and prayer, study of the Bible, practicing the presence of God, and wanting to know God and His will for your life. The Biblical rule is: "Precept must be upon precept, precept upon precept, line upon line, line upon line, here a little, there a little."[6]

The Bible says that the mature, by reason of use, have their senses exercised to discern good from evil. If "good" is the will of God for you, then "evil" must be whatever is not God's plan for you.

If God's plan for you is radiant health, then evil would be the consumption of tobacco or alcohol or excessive fat or rich foods, which would clog your arteries, make you overweight, and hasten your death.

If God's plan for you is achievement and success, then evil would be your becoming an indolent "couch potato," vegetating in front of a television set.

If God's plan for you is a happy Christian marriage, then evil would be to link up with a person who didn't believe in God and might try to ruin your life.

The Life of Brother Lawrence

We can learn from the seventeenth-century writings of a lay brother of the Carmelite Order, Brother Lawrence. After his death in 1691, his "Conversations" and "Letters" were put together in a small book, *Practicing the Presence of God*. This monk was by no means a famous man. Most desk top dictionaries today do not even mention him among the famous people named Lawrence. Yet, he found the secret of joyous eternal life in the midst of mundane temporal life, which has blessed many Christians in later centuries.

Brother Lawrence was part of the monastery's kitchen help, and he learned to practice the presence of God while washing dishes, pots, and pans, while stacking them, while serving food, and performing the most menial tasks of his order.

His writings stress the need to do everything, including

the kitchen work that he naturally disliked, for the love of God. This will lead, he said, to a condition in which the presence of God is as real in work as in prayer. But it requires practice and patience—one step, one minute, at a time. Here's how Brother Lawrence practiced God's presence:

> My soul has an habitual, silent, secret conversation with God. This often causes inward joys and raptures. Outwardly sometimes, too. So much so I am forced to moderate them lest they be seen by others.[7]

Do you see the point? Brother Lawrence knew God was good. He knew His promises. He knew He had promised to be with him always. There was no distinction between sacred and secular. *Everything* he did was to be divine service founded on love, for when Jesus said, "I am with you always," He didn't mean just in the pew or in prayer or in preaching or in song.[8] He included those times, yes, but He meant *always*.

When we go to work, we're working for God, whether we're a salesman, a real estate developer, an oil driller, a farmer, a rancher, a maintenance man, a preacher, or an author. We are to be aware that God is with us at all times; His Spirit is with us forever. And we're to act as though He's with us. We're to listen to Him, introduce Him to others. We can't compartmentalize our lives—religion on this side, no religion on that side.

The world tells us to compartmentalize. In fact, our society is in serious trouble because of this. I knew it years ago, but the presidential campaign of 1988 drove it home relentlessly. How many times—in person, in the papers, on television—was I told that religion and politics do not mix?

God says, "I'm with you always whether you're serving in public office or in the Christian Broadcasting Network or in the Southern Baptist Church." But we have vast numbers of the influential people who are bent upon making the First Amendment of the constitution say something it doesn't say. Their intention is to remove Christianity from American life.

The fact is, if someone is in the plan of God, then God is central in his life. He is at the core of everything. All that person does should be in recognition that God is at the center of the universe. He is behind everything.

So Brother Lawrence was out in the kitchen of the monastery with the pots and pans, but he was performing divine service. He loved the Lord at all times, and he simply told the ever-present Lord that he loved Him, and the ever-present Lord communicated His love to him.

Brother Lawrence lived in God's good plan. However, he, like you and I, could have chosen the opposite.

That Which Is Evil

If God's plan for me was to found a Christian television network, then evil would have been to ignore God's call and play it safe by accepting the pastorate of a sizeable church.

Evil, by that broad definition, *is anything that limits, hinders, or diverts you from God's highest and best for you.*

Good, by the same definition, is whatever lawful act leads you toward the fulfillment of God's plan for you, to become like Jesus Christ and to perform those good works which God "prepared beforehand that we should walk in them."[9]

If ultimate good is God's plan for the world to be united in peace and love under the Lordship of Jesus Christ, then the New Age concept of a world united under the revelation of Satanic "Ascended Masters" must be ultimate evil.

Satan's Plan: The Antichrist

Even as God has a plan, so also does Satan have a plan to unite all mankind under the ultimate horror: the reign of a world dictator known as the Antichrist.

I believe that the time is coming on this earth when Christians will no longer be seeking God's guidance only about education, marriage, employment, investments, housing, church attendance, and the like. I believe that every Christian will be tested as never before by an antichrist deception so powerful and so subtle that all but the strongest Christians will be tempted by the incredible supernatural appeal of the pseudo "Christos Spirit" as they call it.

The New Age Hinduism, motivated by demonic forces, is being taught in our schools, in our businesses, in our motion pictures, and in our television programs. The one repeated message is the need for one world harmony, according to the revelation of those "Masters" who claim to have touched infinity. According to author Tal Brooke in his recent book *When the World Be As One*, these concepts are being embraced at the very highest levels of government and finance.[10]

I recently heard of a Christian couple who were listening to a Christian radio program as they were driving with their young children. The radio speaker began to pray, "Oh God, Thou master of the universe." Just then their little six-year-old boy yelled out from the back seat with all of the wisdom gained from watching New Age television on Saturday morning, "He's wrong. God's not master of the universe, He-Man is!" (In case you are not up on children's television, the program the little boy was referring to has been winning the children's TV ratings sweeps all over the country. It is called "He-Man and the Masters of the Universe.")

Make no mistake about it. Your ability and the ability of your loved ones to discern good from evil will be tested in hundreds of ways in the years ahead. That is why I urge you to learn God's ways now. I also urge you to learn to recover from mistakes of judgment without feelings of guilt and self-condemnation. When you make a mistake, push yourself up, ask *God's forgiveness*, and get on with your life. God knows your weakness. It is not His nature to condemn but to forgive.

The First Struggle Between Good and Evil

The struggle of mankind to discern good from evil goes all the way back to the Garden of Eden. There, God placed the first human beings in a garden of delights: fruit so delicious that men today would kill just for a taste of it; flowers so gorgeous that no painter could ever capture their colors.

Adam and Eve had direct access to God and what was called the "tree of life."[11] Therefore, there could never be sickness, pain, or death in the Garden of Eden.

In the garden, the first people had their physical, aesthetic, and spiritual needs met. To be complete their moral sense needed to be formed and developed as well. So God placed in the garden what was called the "tree of the knowledge of good and evil."[12] Then God gave them only one command, "Of every tree of the garden you may freely eat; but of the fruit of the tree of the knowledge of good and evil you shall not eat."[13]

This was not a magic tree but a symbol that God was using to teach the newly-formed humans to listen to His commands.

I should point out that Adam and Eve had access to hundreds of fruit trees, each one more delicious than the other. They had absolute freedom to do whatever they pleased. *God's way to us is always freedom.* "Where the spirit of the Lord is, there is liberty."[14]

Yet the lie in the garden is the same lie we hear in today's world. There is one tree that is being kept from you. Therefore, God is mean. God is unfair. God is keeping something good from you. God has some ulterior motive.

We hear it now all over the country, "You weird evangelicals represent a God who wants to keep us from reproductive freedom . . . a God who wants to keep us from our own 'choice.'" Doesn't the world's cry for "freedom of choice" against "God's tyranny" ring a bit hollow:

- Now that 24 million unborn babies have been slaughtered?[15]
- Now that one in four Americans have some form of venereal disease including one that always kills?[16]
- Now that 23 million Americans are addicted to illegal narcotics?[17]
- Now that 390,000 Americans are dying each year from smoking tobacco?[18]
- Now that one out of every three homes in the land is cursed by alcoholism?[19]
- Now that 60 million Americans are at risk of heart disease because of too rich a diet?[20]

When will we as a nation tell those pseudo-scientific frauds that eating the forbidden fruit of drugs, permissive and bizarre sex, and violent slaughter of our young lead to the loss of paradise, not to some exalted consciousness?

Those who follow God's will for their lives have an automatic shield against such decadence.

The Option God Gives to Us

God helped Adam and Eve establish a pattern of resisting evil and choosing good. Each day as they walked by the tree they would say to themselves, *Eating this tree is evil. Not eating is good.* Day by day as they went through this routine their senses were being "exercised to discern good and evil."[21] Obeying God's command was good. Not obeying God's command was evil. After a while following God's direction would have become such a part of their nature that they literally could not have broken His command.

The theologians of the Middle Ages described this possibility with two Latin phrases, *Posse non peccare*—able not to sin—then transformed into *Non posse peccare*—not able to sin.

In dealing with God, who is perfect love, we are not faced with situational ethics. It does not matter what we (in hearts and minds that are affected by the world around us) think is good. If we want God's will, we must learn what He calls good, and we must learn what He calls evil. One of the great tragedies of our time is that school children have been deeply immersed in relativism and situational ethics and no longer believe in the absolutes of God. This trend by itself is killing our civilization.

Obviously, we begin to counter this with the Word of God. It is God-breathed, infallible, and unchanging. And by practice, by reason of use, we can learn it.

As I've said, this doesn't happen overnight. I've been walking with the Lord for more than thirty years and I'm still learning the difference between the voice of God and the voices of my clamoring spirit, of the world, and of Satan. My batting average has improved to a fairly consistent level, but I am quick to say, like Paul, that I have not reached the goal. I still repeat the Beazley episode. I may believe something is God's will, and it turns out not to be. It may be an urging of my own will. But I don't enter into condemnation over it. As the saying goes: "Be patient; He isn't finished with me yet."

The same goes for you. He isn't finished with you, so don't expect to be perfect instantly. Just watch a miracle unfold for the rest of your life.

6

Look for Two or More Witnesses

When I was a student in prep school in 1945, I was able to obtain a summer job with the United States Forest Service in the LoLo National Forest on the Idaho border, east of Missoula, Montana. My job was to work as part of a brush disposal crew high up in the Rocky Mountains.

Early each day our crew was trucked up the mountains on logging roads, armed with double-blade axes and crosscut saws to pile up the residue from commercial logging crews, which would minimize the risk of forest fires. Today, I would think it an egregious waste of taxpayers' money for the government to pay crews to clean up after the work of private logging companies who operate in national forests. Then, all I could think of was the back-breaking work and the spectacular scenery. I will never forget lying on a bed of fir needles during our lunch break and looking up at the towering trees and the fleecy clouds floating above them. Even today I can smell that sweet, fresh Rocky Mountain air and the rain-washed smell of the trees.

Our forests are a precious natural resource and their greatest enemy is fire. Fire set by lightning. Fire set by careless motorists. Fire set by campers. And, in 1945, fire set by incendiary balloons which were sent aloft into the prevailing winds by our World War II enemies, the Japanese.

To alert forest workers and volunteers to the onset of fire, the Park Service established a network of strategic lookouts on peaks throughout the forests. These lookout stations were little one-room houses, mounted high in the air, atop four long poles. They afforded clear visibility on all sides. At the center of the lookout station was a large flat disk with precise compass coordinates.

If the worker assigned to the lookout detected smoke or fire, his job was to establish a precise line to the sighting, then report the compass direction to the ranger station in the valley.

Because of the vast distances involved, and the virtual impossibility of estimating distances in the mountains by sight alone, triangulation (pinpointing locations by the intersecting lines) was imperative. In other words, it took a second or even third opinion to get action.

Once two or more calls came in, a ranger could pinpoint the precise coordinates on a map and dispatch fire-fighting crews to the area.

Two or More Witnesses

The Hebrews had the same type of verification system way back in 1300 B.C. Their law code required that no one could be convicted of a crime unless there were two or more witnesses. The wisdom of this law is clear. Witnesses forget. Their perception is blurred. In a traffic accident, for instance, a witness looking at an approaching vehicle gets a totally different view than a person who views the same accident from the side.

That is why Jesus also recommended this spiritual rule. "By the mouth of two or three witnesses every word may be established."[1] The fourth key to receiving God's direction in your life is: *Look for two or more witnesses.*

Since we know that God always follows His own word in the Bible, you can assume that He does not expect you to move out confidently on some aspect of His plan without two or more witnesses to confirm it. You should expect lines of guidance, like those from the forest lookout stations, to intersect precisely to confirm what God is saying to you.

God's Direction to Peter

A classic case of this type of direction is found in the life of the apostle Peter at the time of the beginning of the church.

Up to this time no Gentile had ever received Jesus Christ as Lord and Savior. But God had a plan to begin with Cornelius. Since Jesus had given the keys of the Kingdom to Peter, it would be Peter's privilege first to open the doors to the Jews on the day of Pentecost, then to open the doors to the Gentiles at the house of Cornelius, the captain of a hundred men (a centurion) in Caesarea.

Cornelius was a man who not only prayed regularly but was also very generous with his money. About three o'clock one afternoon, he saw an angel in a vision who gave him specific instructions to send men up the coast to Joppa to contact Simon Peter who was staying at the house of a leather worker named Simon.

About noon the day after the angel had appeared to Cornelius, Peter went up to the flat roof of Simon's house to pray. While he was praying, he became hungry, then he fell into a trance. He began to see in a vision a sheet lowered down from heaven which held pigs, snakes, birds, and other animals that were not kosher for Jews to eat.

Then a voice spoke, "Get up Peter, kill, and eat."

But Peter said, "No, Lord, I have never in my life eaten such creatures, for they are forbidden by our Jewish laws."

Then the voice spoke again, "Don't contradict God. If He says something is kosher, then it is."

This vision was repeated three times in precise detail. An extraordinary emphasis, clearly establishing the truth of the matter.

Peter was perplexed. As often happens this was the first line of God's guidance, and it was not understood by itself. Surely God was not telling him to go out and dine on snakes and eels.

At this precise moment the three messengers from Cornelius arrived at the door of the house. As Peter was standing on the rooftop, puzzling over his three-fold vision, the Holy Spirit within spoke to his inner man, *There are three men downstairs looking for you. Go down and meet them and go with them. All is well, I have sent them.* An inner voice from God was now amplifying slightly what

Peter had seen in the vision. This was the second line of God's direction.

Then Peter went downstairs and there were the three men, just as the inner voice of the Spirit had told him. Indeed, they told him of the angel who had visited Cornelius, and they invited Peter to come with them to Caesarea, just as the Holy Spirit had said.

Now Peter had received a third line of God's direction—circumstances, not known to him by any natural means previously, confirming precisely what the Holy Spirit had said to him a few moments before.

There was even a fourth line of God's direction, for the messengers told Peter that an angel had appeared to Cornelius and had instructed Cornelius to send for Peter that he might receive spiritual assistance.

Yet God had even more confirmation. In His wisdom, He knew that the orthodox Jews in the early church hated Gentiles. He also knew that all their lives they had been taught that contact with Gentiles was every bit as defiling as eating swine's flesh. The Hebrew word for Gentile, *Goyim,* although it technically meant "nations" had come to signify "pagan sinner" to the Jews of Peter's day. The Goyim had for centuries been their enemies, their persecutors, and often the agents of apostasy.

Now God was telling His church to open their doors and their hearts to these pagans. In fact He was to show them that the Gentiles who accepted Jesus Christ as their Savior were to have absolutely equal privileges in His kingdom alongside Jews. We, who live in a world where equality of all races is considered an ideal, may find it hard to understand what a shocking change this concept entailed to the simple and devout Jews of first-century Christianity. They needed massive, supernatural, irrefutable confirmation that the Gentile world was indeed a part of God's plan.

When Peter arrived the next day at Cornelius's house accompanied by other believers, he began to tell about Jesus Christ to those assembled. He mentioned nothing to them about the baptism of the Holy Spirit or the events of Pentecost. Yet, while he was still speaking, the power of the Holy Spirit fell on the assembled Gentiles, and by supernatural power they began to speak in languages not their own.[2]

Peter had now received the most conclusive line of God's direction. The Holy Spirit Himself, without any other human instrument, had come upon these Gentiles at the very moment they believed in Jesus Christ. And He did it in precisely the same fashion that He had empowered the Jewish Christians on the day of Pentecost.

Now Peter understood the vision. Everyone is a candidate for the kingdom of heaven. No nation is to be excluded. How could Jewish Christians any longer reject those that God had cleansed?

By many witnesses, by irrefutable proofs, the thing had been established.

Think what God provided to confirm His plan. A visiting angel, three visions, the inner direction of the Holy Spirit, confirming circumstances, and the outward demonstration of the Holy Spirit before several eye witnesses. Later, when the privileges and duties of the Gentile Christians were being debated before the Church Council in

Jerusalem, Peter won the day by simply reciting the clear proofs that God had given him in the case of Cornelius.

You might say, "Sure, that was the first century and Peter was a famous apostle, how does that affect me?"

The answer is simple. God says, "I am the LORD, I do not change."[3] The God of Moses, of Gideon, of Peter, of Paul is our God today. Note carefully that in the case of Moses, Gideon, Peter, and Paul, God took the initiative to direct His chosen ones to perform that part of His plan, which had been assigned to them. They were not acting like children in the back of the classroom waving their hands so the teacher would call on them; they were not volunteers asking God to endorse "their ministry." God called and they obeyed.

Remember, we have been saved unto good works, "which God prepared beforehand that we should walk in them."[4] He already has selected the works and the tools to do them, so we need to learn the principles of how He will reveal them to us.

The Plan That God Has Ordained for You

Assume the following modern-day scenario as a model for learning a part of God's plan in your life from several intersecting lines of God's direction.

You are a businessman, and your business is prospering. You need to expand your office and warehouse space. Your natural inclination and business experience tell you to find a larger place to lease, so you look diligently but nothing is available. Since you are a man of prayer, you pray about the decision and keep looking. More dead ends.

So you ask your financial people to run cost-benefit and present value studies to compare your cost of leasing versus the possibility of building your own building. The figures look slightly favorable toward building if the cost of money is low. So now you start looking for land—three to five acres would be plenty. More dead ends. Nothing suitable. Your employees are virtually sitting on top of one another. You can't keep up with the growth of your business. You are increasingly frustrated. It seems so easy, why doesn't God help?

Then one day you drive by a major intersection at the center of your city. It is the best piece of undeveloped real estate in your entire area. The bank has just foreclosed on it. All you want is 5 acres and this is 140 acres. It is far too big a deal for a little guy like you, so you drive on by.

The next morning before you leave the house, God speaks to you. *I want you to buy that 140 acres. You can build your business, you can build a shopping mall, and you can dedicate land to build a church.*

Your heart jumps. This land is worth millions, and you can't afford it. But if this was God's voice, maybe it can happen.

The issue burning inside of you is simple: *Was this my own mind taking me on a massive ego trip, or did I really hear from God?* You need confirmation.

On the way to work you drive by the property. You get out and walk around, praying silently. You "check your gut." Inside you is a deep peace. This thing feels right.

But you aren't about to gamble your life savings on an

inner voice and a good feeling. You need something hard. Tangible. Outside of your subjective experience.

When you walk into your office, your business manager comes in with you and shuts the door. "You know, I have an idea. We need land, and I heard last night that the bank foreclosed on 140 of the best acres in town. I think we could build our new building, then we could make a bundle on the rest with a shopping center. We could even donate some land to build a church."

Obviously, you don't want to let him know that he has been reading your mind, so you act surprised. "That is really far out," you say, "but I try to keep an open mind. Why don't you check out the details from the bank?"

When your business manager walks out of your office, you look up at the ceiling with a grin. *Lord,* you say, *I believe You may be telling me something.*

Your business manager comes back a couple of days later. "The land is appraised for $2.8 million," he says matter-of-factly. "The equity holders have taken a bath for $500,000, and the bank will sell its interest for $2.3 million."

This price is much less than you had imagined. So now it is time to use the mind and the training God has given you. You begin to analyze the cost structure of the deal. How much would the payments on the land be? What would the development costs be? What would the square footage rental of a future shopping center be? How much money would you receive by selling off choice outparcels at retail? You factor in the rapidly appreciating price of land in that area, and you find out about planned highway improvements for the future.

When you are finished it is obvious that all of the numbers check out. This is not a good deal, it is a sensational deal. But you know that sensational deals can go sour. If it was that sensational why did the previous owners go bankrupt?

If the thing is of God, you want to go forward. If not, you can keep on looking. You now have intersecting confirming points. One, the voice of the Spirit of God. Two, the peace of God in your heart. Three, confirming circumstances from your business manager and from your own business analysis. But you still want more before you act.

The next day as you are reading the Bible and seeking further confirmation, a verse of Scripture jumps at you as if it is printed in bold face type: "Today you are going to know for sure that the living God is among you and He will, without fail, drive out . . . all the people who now live in *the land you will soon occupy*."⁵

This word may have been for Joshua, but God just gave it to you as well. You know that God has truly spoken, and that He has confirmed without a doubt His will for you.

Has God spoken to the bankers as well? you wonder. To make the deal successful, the bank needs to make major concessions. What you don't know is that bank examiners are on the way and the bank is just as anxious to clear non-performing loans as you are to buy the property.

In God's plan don't ever feel pressured. As my friend Harald Bredesen likes to say, make it "hard on God and easy on yourself."

So you call the bank. It turns out that the official handling the disposition of the land is a friend. You tell him your story, then you ask the impossible. "I will buy the land," you hear yourself saying, "for nothing down, interest only for two years, and the balance over twenty-three years at 8 percent simple interest."

"Is that all?" the banker asks.

"Yes," you reply, "that's all I can think of."

"Well, I think that we can accommodate you."

The deal is signed and becomes more profitable than you possibly could have imagined as land values go up 1000 percent in the years you hold the property.

This is precisely the way God can and does lead people today in the everyday details of their lives. I know because, with some changes for instructional purposes, the story of the land purchase I have just told you about actually happened to me and CBN when we bought our present site in 1975.

I can look back on hundreds of examples like this, times when I have experienced the clear, precise leading of God. Had I not obeyed God in 1959 to leave Brooklyn with seventy dollars to buy a television station, there would have been no CBN. No "700 Club" program. No university. No Operation Blessing. No Middle East television. Over one million people might not have met the Lord, and over 30 million people might not have been clothed or fed.

I have never been afraid to take chances. One suggested title for my autobiography of those early days *(Shout It from the Housetops)* was *I Gambled on God.* It is one thing to take a chance at age twenty-nine when you have nothing. It is something else to take a chance at age fifty-six and leave a national organization with two thousand employees and combined annual revenues approaching $200 million.

The Witness of Three Million Signatures

God had spoken to me for years about his wishes in regard to the presidency.

There were many specific confirming scriptures. There were Christians who claimed to have heard from God. There were secular Conservatives urging a run. There were literally thousands upon thousands of people in rallies across America on their feet yelling, "Go for it, Pat."

More dramatically, I had laid before the Lord a specific "fleece," as I mentioned in chapter 3. If God had not willed me to run, He could have left the hurricane alone in 1985; it would have hit our region and I would have been out of politics the very next day.

Once in my early Christian days, a Billy Graham training director said, "God will move heaven and earth to keep you from being misled." So when there is doubt about positive guidance, it is always possible to pray for negative guidance. This I prayed, over and over again, "Father, I only want Your will. Please, please don't let me be misled."

Elijah's Showdown

During the summer of 1986 I was reading the story of Elijah's famous showdown with the priests of Baal on

Mount Carmel. He desired to demonstrate to the people that God was true and Baal was false. His challenge was simple, "The God who answers by sending fire is the true God."[6]

When his turn came, Elijah carefully laid out wood and a sacrifice on the altar. If he had been like some miracle workers I have heard of, he might have been inclined to slip a few coals under the fire to help God out. In fact, most of us have a tendency to give God a hand whenever we can.

But not Elijah. He called for barrels of water and poured them on. Then he did it again. Then again. The sacrifice was soaked, the wood was soaked, and water had collected in a ditch around the altar. Elijah didn't make it hard for God, he made it virtually impossible!

Then he prayed, "Let it be known this day that I have done all these things at Your word."[7] Fire fell from heaven. The wood, the sacrifice, the water, even the stones, were consumed in an instant.[8] Elijah's call was from God. There was no confusion in anyone's mind.

By 1986, I had received all the guidance that a man of faith needed to proceed on the course God had laid out for me. I could have continued my work quietly until the fall of 1987, and then announced for the presidency.

Instead, I came up with a plan, modeled after Elijah's challenge. I wanted to make this one hard for God and easy on me. I had my own equivalent of three barrels of water. I was going to ask for a miracle of support from the Christians of America, not for a sign from God for myself because I had that. On September 17, 1986, the two hundredth year of the signing of the Constitution of the United States, I announced from Constitution Hall in Washington to a closed circuit network of over two hundred locations across America that if 3 million people would sign petitions of support for my candidacy by September 17, 1987, I would announce as a candidate for the Republican party's nomination for the presidency of the United States. If not, I would withdraw from the race without ever becoming a candidate.

I felt that the plan was brilliant. I could continue to serve CBN on television while a parallel organization raised the money, assembled the mailing list, and recruited more volunteers than any campaign in history. I figured that 6 million people were needed to win the nomination. If I had identified 3 million supporters in advance in the right states, and they would enlist just one more person each, the nomination theoretically would have been won in advance. If I did not obtain the signatures, then I could continue my work at CBN with no damage to me or the network.

Testing the Waters

We took off like a rocket, but fizzled about as quickly as a misfired firecracker. The apparatus to gather 3 million signatures was not in place and nothing was happening, except the many bills that piled up from the gala opening and the initial mailings. In retrospect, the plan was brilliant, but with man's brilliance, not God's. It was as if Jesus Christ had told the Father that He would go to the cross only if He were guaranteed in advance that 3 million people would become born-again Christians the first year after His crucifixion.

Once my announcement was made, I was working under the auspices of "Americans for Robertson," a Federal Election Committee, "Testing the Waters" organization. All the money spent during those twelve months—$10 million in all—counted against my total federal spending limit of $30 million—and when I needed money for television in 1988 it just wasn't there. If we had been able to organize a campaign structure in every early primary state to mobilize volunteer supporters in numbers equal to vote goals from those states, our success would have been inevitable. Instead, we had no organization and we encountered incredible difficulty just putting it all together. Months dragged by and money poured out. What I thought would have been an easy boost to a future campaign became a costly anchor. I could not announce without the 3 million signatures, and by early summer of 1987 we weren't even close.

By the end of August, it looked as if we weren't going to make it. My integrity was at stake, even though it was my show and I was perfectly free to choose the rules. There had never been enough time or structure to permit obtaining signatures as I had wanted, so telephoning various lists to line up supporters seemed just as acceptable.

The names were now pouring in, 15,000 to 35,000 a day, but it did not seem that we were going to make it by our target of September 17, 1987.

Once again I went before the Lord in earnest prayer. "Lord," I prayed, "I know that You want me to do this, but without 3 million names I cannot go forward. If this is what You want me to do, I must have a miracle. Otherwise I am out."

Crossing the Last Hurdle

Then the miracle happened. A person that I am not at liberty to identify, without realizing how desperate we were, sent to us, for appropriate consideration if we needed them, a list of 3 million names and addresses of people who would be sympathetic to my candidacy. As we called these people we learned that about 75 percent would be willing to support me for President.

I hadn't wanted another sign, but God had supplied it just the same. The 3 million names made our goal certain of realization even though our own recruiting efforts were still being tabulated.

When September 17 arrived, we had over 5 million names at our headquarters. Leaving out the 3 million names from the special "miracle" list, which we never used, our final computer print out (which was not perfected until the end of 1988) showed the names of 1,800,000 households where there were 3 million people!

God had done His part—and on time. I had a miracle answer to confirm His plan for me to run.

Unfortunately, I didn't have the time or the money to process more than a small portion of the huge volume of people, get them organized by precinct, and contact them on a state-by-state basis. I asked for names of people. God gave them to me. Some proved enormously helpful.

Others will be there to help another candidate on another day.

In any event, the last hurdle had been crossed. The last line of my intersecting guidance had been laid down. On September 17, 1987, I announced that I was "going for it." Then on October 1, 1987, I resigned my post as president of CBN and before a backdrop of bands, bunting, and balloons I announced to cheering capacity crowds in Manchester, New Hampshire; Des Moines, Iowa; and Dallas, Texas, that I was an official candidate for the Republican nomination for the presidency of the United States.

The wait was over. The race had begun. I had obeyed what I felt was God's clear leading in my life. My life would never be the same again.

7

Know the Bible

The highlight of my bid for the presidential nomination took place on February 8, 1988 in the state of Iowa. Both the Republican party and the Democratic party considered the Iowa caucuses the first major tests of the field of candidates. The nation's media poured into Iowa.

In Iowa I had a quality organization working in all ninety-nine counties. The literature was on target. Connie Snapp, our communications director, had done an outstanding job saturating Iowa television and radio with quality spot advertising.

Marlene Elwell, my Iowa campaign manager, realized that we were not just fighting a political battle but a spiritual battle as well, so she organized prayer chains of daily intercessors all over the state.

I had personally visited churches, factories, home parties, rallies in airports, shopping centers, offices, and lodge halls. My wife, Dede, and I had ridden horseback in a parade in Spencer, Iowa, in 102-degree weather. In January and February we organized two statewide whistle-stop bus tours. One started in Davenport, Iowa, on the eastern side of the state and went to Shenandoah on the western side, then slightly north and back across the state again.

The temperature in Spencer in the summer had been plus 102 degrees; the wind chill temperature that day in February was minus 60 degrees. I spoke as many as thirteen times a day, often in blowing snow, shook hands, and greeted the people. One of the thrills was to have top country-western singer Ricky Skaggs with me along with a lovely Christian girl, Randall Brooks, who had sung the lead in the Broadway show, "Annie."

Iowa was textbook perfect. It was a campaign of fresh, eager people, organized to perfection, who were working their hearts out under the leadership of a highly spiritual, highly motivated professional.

When the results were in, my good friend Senator Bob Dole from Kansas had won, to nobody's surprise. What shocked the nation was the fact that a religious leader who was a political novice and an extreme underdog had trounced the sitting vice president of the United States and heir-apparent to Ronald Reagan. The morning headlines did not say, "Dole Wins Iowa." Instead they trumpeted, "Robertson Beats Bush."

With only two weeks to go before the New Hampshire primary, I headed east to that tiny bastion of freedom known as "The Granite State."

New Wine in Old Wineskins

I had thought there was also a strong organization in New Hampshire. My area director glowingly reported we had almost 20,000 names on the mailing list, a statewide precinct organization in place, and strong showings in shopping center polls. We were also sponsoring exciting home parties, door-to-door visitation, and media coverage.

With less than three months before the primary, I discovered that his enthusiasm got the better of him. The size of the mailing list was a fraction of what had been claimed. The organization was virtually nonexistent, and I had the highest negatives of any candidate in New Hampshire history.

In desperation I looked for an established political leader who was a political conservative and a professed Christian. Former governor of New Hampshire Meldrin Thompson seemed an excellent choice, but he was supporting former Senator Paul Laxalt of Nevada. Then, when Paul dropped out, Mrs. Nackey Loeb, the feisty publisher of the *Manchester Union Leader*, asked her friend Mel Thompson to assist former UN Ambassador Jeane Kirkpatrick in a possible run. Jeane Kirkpatrick is a brilliant scholar and conservative thinker who agonized over her decision for several weeks and then said no to former Governor Thompson. Now Governor Thompson said yes to me.

Governor Thompson threw himself into the task with gusto. He was campaign manager, scheduler, and a man who watched every dollar spent. His experience in campaigning had been in statewide general elections with secular candidates. He had never had to deal with a presidential primary and a candidate who was a religious leader.

We ran a campaign not based on precinct organization

but on my personality as a candidate. The goal was to shake fifteen hundred hands a day in supermarkets, factories, restaurants, offices. However, I was running in a Republican primary, and by law in New Hampshire, Democrats can't vote in a Republican primary. In short, my last two months in New Hampshire were being put together as if I were running for governor of the state in a general election, which mirrored Thompson's personal experience. By the time we got through in New Hampshire I had to explain my way out of the short end of a near tie for last.

I had already won 82 percent of the Hawaii delegates. I was the real winner in Michigan, although the final delegates were denied me. Both Bob Dole and I had beaten George Bush in Iowa, Kansas, and South Dakota. We knew we had him beat in Minnesota. Dole had come into New Hampshire with a slight lead over Bush. The only chance any of the other candidates had was for Dole to win in New Hampshire. My hope was for a Dole victory in New Hampshire to derail Bush. I only needed a strong third place finish. Then I would have been positioned to pick up weakening Bush support in southern states like Virginia, Texas, and Louisiana where I was ahead of Dole. Then hope for a miracle in the far west so that at the convention there would have been an opportunity to negotiate with Dole for a win.

I was staying down the hall from Bob Dole at the Hilton Hotel. On the Sunday before the Tuesday primary, his pollster, Fred Wirthlin, brought him the bad news: With two days to go he had slipped to second behind Bush. His staff was up all night frantically trying to fix a new schedule, but they were too late. The forces of Governor John Sununu, who was Bush's campaign manager and now his White House Chief of Staff, were just too strong. On primary day George Bush swept the state.

I awoke early on the morning after the New Hampshire primary, and reached for the Bible. As I looked at the open page my heart jumped, "Nor do people put new wine into old wineskins, or else the wineskins break, the wine is spilled, and the wineskins are ruined. But they put new wine into new wineskins, and both are preserved."[1]

I understood clearly what went wrong in New Hampshire. My campaign was the fresh new wine of eager volunteers, filled with moral fervor seeking to make a better world for themselves and their children. My strength had been a carefully crafted door-to-door precinct organization, carried out by thousands of volunteers. And above all else my strength in Iowa had come from the earnest, continuous prayer of dedicated prayer warriors.

I had tried to pour all that into the old wineskins of worked-over, conservative New Hampshire Republican politics. In the process the old skins were torn and damaged and the new wine was lost.

Unfortunately for me, this revelation came after the fact, not before.

But the guidance was there for me. I knew the Bible, and I should have known that my desperate move in New Hampshire was biblically unsound. Had I followed what I should have known, I could have achieved a strong third, which is all I expected, and a better chance in the South.

I went into the South courageously. Regretfully, the

game was over. The narrow window opened by Iowa had slammed shut.

God Communicates with People

My point in raising these events is to illustrate an important principle in seeking and receiving God's guidance. The Bible clearly says the Lord has many ways of communicating with people. For example, the letter to the Hebrews opens with these words: "God, who at various times and in different ways spoke in time past to the fathers by the prophets, has in these last days spoken to us by His Son."[2]

The wonder of that passage is the awesome truth that Almighty God, creator of heaven and earth, *speaks* to His people, which includes us. He spoke in ancient times by inspiring prophets through the Holy Spirit, and Paul says those "sacred writings" were preserved so we might receive instruction. The fifth key to receiving God's direction in your life is: *Know the Bible*.

Scripture: 95 Percent of Our Guidance

For you and for me, God does not depend on cloudy visions, uncertain voices, and questionable circumstances to reveal His will to us.

The apostle Paul told his disciple Timothy, "All scripture is given by inspiration of God, and is profitable for doctrine, for reproof, for correction, for instruction in righteousness."[3]

Probably 95 percent of all the guidance we need as Christians is found in the clearly understood principles of the Holy Bible.

We don't need a revelation from God to tell us that sex outside of marriage is wrong. The Bible says, "You shall not commit adultery."[4] It also says emphatically, "Flee sexual immorality."[5]

We don't need an angel to tell us not to kill or steal. Two commandments clearly say, "You shall not murder,"[6] and, "You shall not steal."[7] As Ted Koppel said so eloquently, "God gave us the Ten Commandments, not the Ten Suggestions."

We don't need a church council to ordain homosexuals. The Bible clearly says, "You shall not lie with a male as with a woman. It is an abomination."[8] (How can any church claim they have God's mandate to ordain what God calls an abomination?)

We don't need a special "leading" to give tithes to the Lord. The Bible says those who withhold tithes are thieves, robbing God.[9]

You don't need special guidance to go to church, love your neighbor as yourself, stop making a god out of money, stop cheating your employees or your employers.

Husbands and wives don't need a special vision to avoid divorce. The Bible says, God "hates divorce."[10] Nor do we need an audible command to love one another. The Bible says, "Husbands, love your wives, just as Christ also loved the church,"[11] and "Wives, submit to your own husbands as is fitting unto the Lord."[12]

Certain books in the Bible, like the book of Proverbs, are literally blueprints for business management, employee-employer relations, government, personal growth and development, and child care.

Some people overlook these relevant passages because a few parts of the Bible do not apply to us today. We eat bacon with our eggs with no guilt, because Jesus cleansed all foods. We no longer offer animal sacrifice, because Jesus is our perfect sacrifice. We are not under new moons and festivals and sabbaths, because these are merely Old Testament symbols of the reality in Jesus. We do not launch wars of extermination, because Jesus told us to love our enemies.

The Way I Operate

People often ask me how I use the Bible in my daily life. The answer is quite simple. I rise at least two hours ahead of any activity to read the Bible and pray, a habit I began early in my Christian life and one that I continued even during the rigors and madness of political campaign.

I often kneel when I pray, and many times I simply sit with the Bible open in front of me. God frequently leads me to passages as I pray, and He speaks comfort, consolation, and instruction.

There is no substitute for careful, informed study of the Bible. Read it not for proof texts, but book by book in context, noting who is writing about what to whom. A modern translation is essential so that you can understand what the text says, and, beyond that, a concordance of the Bible so you can find out what the Greek or Hebrew words of the original actually mean.

Remember also that the Holy Spirit is the Author of the

Bible and He is the best exegete of biblical truth. Jesus said, "When He, the Spirit of truth, has come He will guide you into all truth."[13] So be sure to ask for the guiding of the Holy Spirit.

The Bible is what the Germans call "Holy History"—the record of God's dealing with those chosen to bring God's salvation to the world. It records:

- The way God spoke to people.
- How He led people.
- What pleased Him and what displeased Him.

In the Bible we see real flesh and blood human beings like you and me interacting with God and God's plan in their lives.

We watch Abraham, the "friend of God," fudge the truth about his wife because of fear. We see Moses, who spoke face-to-face with God, become angry and dishonor God by striking a rock. We see David, a man after God's own heart, who would carry out God's plan, commit adultery with a voluptuous woman in a moment of weakness. We hear the great apostle Peter deny his Lord before a little servant girl.

We learn from their mistakes. We learn from their successes. We learn the ways of God in His dealing with all of us.

Many times in my years of knowing the Lord I have asked Him for a special word that will be applicable to a particular need I have for guidance. When I first accepted Jesus Christ, I literally pored over the Bible. But I also found that God in His goodness would often guide my hand just to open the Bible and there I would find a verse or passage of scripture that would speak precisely to my need. These "special" scriptures were so amazingly relevant that I knew they had to be sent from God.

Later, after I had received the baptism of the Holy Spirit, I found that God's Spirit would speak quietly to my spirit the name of a book in the Bible and the chapter and verse that I needed to guide me. Some call this a *rhema,* or spoken personal revelation, as opposed to the timeless written *logos* of universal revelation.*

I can assure you that the Holy Spirit of God will never "guide" a person to violate a clear command of the Holy Bible. The inviolability of scripture is so powerful that Jesus Christ declared, "The Scripture cannot be broken."[14] The apostle Paul went further when he said, "Even if we, or an angel from heaven, preach any other gospel to you than what we have preached to you, *let him be accursed.*"[15]

Violating the Principles: The McCloskey Affair

One of the biggest mistakes in my life took place during the presidential campaign when I violated two clear biblical principles: "As much as it depends on you, live at peace with all men,"[16] and another, "Do not avenge yourselves; . . . for it is written, 'Vengeance is Mine, I will repay,' says the Lord."[17] Here is the story:

---

*A word study of the Greek uses of these two words in the New Testament does not support this distinction, but it makes a convenient shorthand for some even if based on questionable scholarship.

In 1981, former California Congressman Pete Mc-
Closkey was attacked by the ·California branch of the
Moral Majority for being "soft on communism." Mc-
Closkey was a decorated Marine Corps veteran of the Ko-
rean War, yet by 1972 his politics had turned to the left. In
that year he appeared on the "Today" show and committed what seemed to me to be an act of treason by suggest-
ing to General Giap of North Vietnam that he stake American prisoners of war in the villages of North Vietnam to
prevent the United States from bombing them.

When the Moral Majority hit him for his statement,
McCloskey went after the Moral Majority by attacking me
because he thought (incorrectly) that I was a member of
this political group. In response to the Moral Majority's
attack on his national loyalty, McCloskey attacked my pa-
triotism by making the unfounded accusation that I had
"used my father's political influence to avoid combat in
Korea in 1951."

Upon my graduation from college in 1950, I was
awarded a commission in a parallel ceremony as a second
lieutenant in the United States Marine Corps Reserve. I
had previously volunteered to join the Marines and had
spent two very hot summers prior to graduation at the
Marine Corps school in Quantico, Virginia.

After a brief summer at the University of London, I
returned home expecting to enter Yale Law School. Instead, the war in Korea had broken out, and in early October I received orders to report what was termed the First
Special Basic Class at Quantico. After less than ninety
days of training, we were given a brief Christmas vaca-

tion, followed by orders to report to San Diego, California, for assignment to the Far East.

I sailed on a troop ship in January of 1951 and arrived in Japan in February. I was twenty years old at the time, and for reasons known only to the Marine Corps, I was assigned to what was called the First Provisional Casual Company at Camp Otsu, Japan, for a period of four months. There I was engaged in rehabilitation training of troops on the way to Korea. I also progressed in my own training to the designation of Combat Infantry Platoon Leader.

In May of 1951, I was transferred to Korea and because of my high verbal skills on the I.Q. test was assigned by a captain at the forward assignment tent to the post of assistant division adjutant. Later, I was moved into the combat zone at the forward division headquarters of the First Marine Division on the border of North Korea. I received three combat battle stars for my service and was rotated on regular schedule back to the United States in 1952 where for a time I served as legal officer, Headquarters Battalion, Marine Corps Schools.

I wrote McCloskey and said that his charge was completely untrue and in fact was libelous. He wrote back that he, in essence, remembered more about my conversations with my father than I did and that he was certain that I had telephoned my father, a United States senator, from the docks in war torn Japan. I wrote back protesting that a dockside telephone call from Japan to the United States in 1950 was an impossibility. And there the matter rested, or so I thought, until McCloskey made the charge again in 1986.

Learning the Hard Way

In 1981, no one of any consequence paid any attention to the story. In 1986, a letter from McCloskey outlining his charges against me was sent to six columnists. All refused to print it. A seventh, Robert Novak of the nationally syndicated Evans and Novak column, who was an ardent supporter of presidential candidate Jack Kemp, printed McCloskey's accusations that I had used my dad's political connections to avoid combat duty. Then Novak quoted McCloskey, who said that I once wrote him, "Making no objections" to his story. "But now Robertson is objecting," reported Novak. "That raises a question of veracity that puts his presidential candidacy on the line."

I could not believe that Novak had quoted McCloskey without calling me to verify his story. The truth was that I *had* objected vigorously to McCloskey's story in my letter to him, calling it "untrue and libelous."

Soon after, I received a call from a Washington friend, advisor, and political expert.

"Is this thing true?" he asked.

"Of course not," I replied.

"I have found," he went on, "that the American people will give you the benefit of the doubt for a time, but if a charge is not rebutted they will come to believe it is true. You have no choice but to sue to prove the falsity of the charge."

Later, I called another friend, a brilliant political expert, and a dedicated Christian, Chuck Colson. I told him the same story. Chuck replied, "It is not the charges against you that people are concerned with, but your reaction to them. Issue a denial of this thing and move ahead. Don't sue."

McCloskey's charge somehow got to me. It was mean and untrue. At stake was not just my reputation and my effectiveness at CBN but the honor of my father, a distinguished United States senator. Yet refuting a lie from thirty years past is virtually impossible.

What I feared more than this charge was what would happen to me if people in the press like Bob Novak felt that I would not call them to account for libel against me. I knew the partisans among them would declare open season on me.

Yet I made one more attempt at settlement. In the summer of 1986, I wrote Pete McCloskey and explained that he was in error and that his statements were injuring me. I asked for a reasonable apology for his baseless attacks. He ignored my letter. I prayed over the matter for a couple of months.

I wanted the truth to come out. Since I knew McCloskey was wrong, I thought he would back down because all I needed from him was a letter of apology. On October 21, 1986, I entered suit against him in the Federal District Court in the District of Columbia and asked for $30 million in damages. I made two serious mistakes in judgment. First, I felt that the press in the United States would report the proceeding fairly. How wrong I was. Not only were they not fair, but they used this case as an occasion to embarrass and humiliate an evangelical minister.

On one occasion my attorneys told me *The Washington Post* actually printed only the portion of the official transcripts that had been underlined for them by McCloskey's lawyer. They would not print one word from the same transcript that gave my side of the case; the story in question ended where my side of the case began.

Since all the evidence was part of a court record, the press could now report every statement (true or false) of every witness with complete immunity. As I read the material, I felt like a character in a Kafka novel. My Marine Corps service record awarded me three battle stars, two for "action against the enemy in Korea." A Marine Corps general, who served with me, said that my duty station was "in combat." Yet almost every week I would read another story saying I had used "political influence to avoid combat."

My second mistake was in believing that justice will prevail in a civil case under the Federal Rules of Civil Procedure. Unfortunately, the deposition process under the Federal Rules became an open hunting ground for a highly partisan lawyer. Teamed with an adversarial press, the process was a nightmare.

My attorneys finally got a videotape of McCloskey admitting under oath that he had never heard me tell anyone of a phone call to the States; they also had obtained in depositions under oath an admission from one of McCloskey's key witnesses that a crucial fact in his previous testimony was not true. Finally, they went to the West Coast and Japan to locate U.S. military personnel formerly stationed in Kobe and Yokosuka, who gave first-hand, convincing testimony that telephone calls described by two other McCloskey witnesses could not possibly have taken place in 1951. After a year-and-a-half of grueling, expensive work we had enough evidence to win the case, but the Federal Judge refused to move it from March 8, 1988—the date of the crucial Super Tuesday presidential primary.

So I was given a choice: Stop campaigning and·throw over the millions of dollars spent on the campaign and the work of hundreds of thousands of loyal people in order to spend two weeks prior to March 8 in preparation for trial. Or dismiss the case, lose the money spent, and listen to McCloskey, who knew he was beaten, gloat publicly that I had "chickened out."

All that anguish could have been avoided by following one simple rule, *"As much as it depends on you, live at peace with all men."*[18] God would have vindicated me. A trial would not.

Another Chance

All of us can remedy our mistakes by responding differently the next time. God gave me that chance after I returned to CBN from the campaign. Our University Board of Regents was furious because the American Bar Association had rejected the application of our Law School for ABA accreditation. A majority of our regents and the school administration wanted us to sue the ABA on civil rights and antitrust grounds. I told them the Mc-Closkey horror story and said I would vote against a lawsuit.

When a second ABA site team turned us down, I again counseled moderation.

Finally, in May of 1989, a third site team inspected our program. This time the team approved our application, the ABA Council on Legal Education added their approval, and the ABA Board of Governors added theirs. On June 15, 1989, CBN University Law School peacefully became the only accredited evangelical law school of its type in America.

My two mistakes did not happen because I did not know the Bible. Nor were they the result of willful disobedience. I would not disobey the Word of God.

Instead, I failed because I chose to believe that the particular circumstances involved (the larger strategies, the counselors, the exigency of the moment) pointed to another course of action as being from God.

I believed that any rational human being making unfounded charges would negotiate an immediate settlement rather than risk financial ruin and a legal bill in the hundreds of thousands of dollars. All I needed or wanted from McCloskey was a simple letter stating that in light of subsequent facts he now realized that his charges were unsubstantiated. I offered arbitration with no damages just to get the truth. The problem was McCloskey did not appear to behave in a rational manner in this case. Once the battle was joined, I was locked in combat with a man who seemed driven by irrational impulses which neither I nor my attorneys could understand.

The moral of the story is simple. *No strategy, no grand design, no emergency, no pressure can supersede the clear word of God*. If you understand it, do it. Leave the rest to the Lord.

8

Let God's Peace Be Your Umpire

In 1964, I drove into the main entrance of Norfolk Motors, owned by a longtime friend, Walter Wilkins. There he was, standing in the middle of the showroom in front of a sparkling new Oldsmobile. He spotted me and waved, heading in my direction as I parked in front of the building.

"Hey, Pat, how goes it?" He was always friendly, ready with a big chuckle.

"Things are great," I said. "What's new?"

There was the chuckle. "Same as always. It's a wonderful life."

He glanced toward my old car. "What can I do for you?"

I smiled and shook my head. "My car's giving me a lot of trouble," I answered, "and I really need another one—I mean, it's bad."

He looked again at the tired Rambler.

"I'd like to trade it in one of your new compacts," I said, not sure I could afford one. But I needed to do something. "What would the difference be?"

Walter, a very good friend and rather wealthy, looked expansively toward his son, James, who had walked up. "James, go get one of the Oldsmobile station wagons, and let's see what Pat thinks of it."

I knew without looking that I'd be going in way over my head if I tried to buy one of the very big popular wagons.

But Walter kept talking, "We can take his little car in on trade, and we'll mark the difference up to the Lord."

I couldn't believe what I was hearing. It turned out to be a white, nine-passenger Oldsmobile 88, a marvelous car with red leather seats and every accessory imaginable. I had not been accustomed to such automotive luxury.

Before the day was out, I drove off in that beauty, still shaking my head at Walter's generosity. I'd heard that he had provided cars to some other ministers in town and that, in some cases, he gave them a new one every year.

A few months later, I picked up a visiting friend and, when he praised the beauty of my new car, I told him that "God provided it. And furthermore," I explained, "there's a good possibility I'll be getting a new one every year."

I don't believe pride or materialism had gripped me, but I recall that I was simply praising the Lord. Instantly, something happened to me inside. My stomach did flip-flops, and I was very uneasy.

I rethought what I'd been saying. After a couple of seconds, I said, "Brother, I'll have to retract that statement, because maybe I won't get a car every couple of years."

Very quickly, the flip-flops and the uneasiness were gone. I know now that, in those few moments and in a relatively minor matter, I had lost the peace of God within my heart. What I didn't know—but God did—was that my friend would sell his dealership before a trade would be .possible. He was as generous as ever, but no longer in a position to favor me or any other minister with a new car every year.

You see, I didn't know the future, but the Holy Spirit did, and I was telling something that wasn't true. And God's peace lifted as He said in effect, "You're not going to walk down that road; you're going to go another way."

Indeed, I would drive that Oldsmobile 88 station wagon well over one hundred thousand miles.

God's Guidance System

This is a very simple demonstration of God's internal guidance system for His people. Mighty ships and mighty airplanes criss-cross oceans and continents daily, depending on highly sophisticated guidance systems. Some depend on inertial guidance, some on the Doppler effect, some on other systems.

How many times have you leaned back in your seat and dozed off peacefully, confident that the plane would reach your correct destination? You didn't give a second thought to the instruments upon which you had placed your faith.

Well, God—being God—is in control of all those systems, and He's in control of the one that's available to His individual followers. The Lord has placed a navigational system within human beings. Like other things, it requires usage and practice.

Paul wrote to the Colossians about it: "Let the peace of God rule in your hearts, to which also you were called in one body; and be thankful."[1]

The sixth key to receiving God's direction in your life is: *Let God's peace be your internal guidance system.* The peace of God is the Christian's compass and gyroscope through life.

Our Compass and Our Gyroscope

This June it was my pleasure as part of a spiritual seminar to host a dinner for some seven hundred of CBN's West Coast supporters aboard the ocean liner, the *Queen Mary,* now in permanent dry dock at Long Beach, California. The *Queen Mary* is huge, measuring three football field lengths from stem to stern. From her keel to the top of her stacks must be at least ten stories in height. This ship carried a reported nineteen thousand troops on one voyage from the United States to Europe during World War II.

I made the voyage from Southampton, England, to New York City aboard the *Queen Mary* during her heyday in 1950. Two days out of New York we hit the tail end of a hurricane in the North Atlantic, and that gigantic vessel rolled from side to side until it seemed to me that the upper decks were on their sides about to skim the surface of the water.

Deep in the bowels of that enormous craft was a device called a gyroscope, meant to keep the vessel level and bring it back to level despite the roughest seas it would encounter. Without a compass and a gyroscope the *Queen Mary* would have wallowed aimlessly about in that cold and hostile ocean. With the compass and the gyroscope she maintained what is called "an even keel" as she majestically cut through the water toward her destination.

Now her engines are quiet. Her propellers no longer turn in the water behind her. She has taken her last voyage. No compass is needed for direction. No gyroscope to steady her course.

Find God's Peace

Unlike the *Queen Mary,* our journey is not over. All of us are en route from our birth to our death. Some are traveling faster than others. Some travel in safe, calm, well-charted waters. Others seem destined to venture forth as pioneers into uncharted and often turbulent waters. Some seem to be speeding over vast distances with singleness of purpose. Others seem to be wallowing in the water or steaming in circles.

God has a chart available for your journey, and He reveals small stages to you as you follow on course.

Wherever your part of God's master plan takes you, God has built into you a gyroscope to keep your life on an even keel. It is called "God's peace." Jesus said to His disciples, just before He departed from them, "Peace I leave with you. My peace I give to you; not as the world gives do I give to you. Let not your heart be troubled, neither let it be afraid."[2]

Some years ago, Dave Garroway, the first host of the *Today* television show, would open each morning with a hand outstretched and the solemn intonation of "Peace!"

In the sixties, the long-haired flower children of America's counter-culture led peace marches and cried out, "Make love not war!"

This is not what Jesus was referring to—an absence of hostility between people and between nations. Jesus was conferring on His disciples a supernatural calm in their Spirit or inner being. This type of spiritual well-being prompted the poet Browning to write, "God's in His Heaven, all's right with the world."[3]

God's Peace Never Fails

When Jesus sent His disciples out two-by-two throughout the Judean countryside, He instructed them to live off the land. If, however, people shared their homes with the disciples, Jesus told them, "First say, 'Peace to this house' and if a son of peace is there, your peace will rest on it; if not it will return to you."[4]

This peace was a tangible thing. The recipient could feel and experience its presence; the sender could feel it leave and return. This deep feeling of rightness, wholeness, and spiritual well-being could not be conferred upon a person by the world. As the gospel song puts it, "The world didn't give it, and the world can't take it away."

The peace of God does not depend on outward circumstances—your position, your power, your money, your success, or your reputation.

Obviously, a feeling of excitement occurs when you receive a promotion or an award or when you are successful in business and land a big order or when your son scores the winning points for his team. Yet the world can steal that satisfaction by taking away that reward. The promotion never comes, the big order is cancelled, your son accidently charges into a defensive player standing in front of the basket. If the good things of the world can give you a high, then the bad things of the world can give you a low.

How many people are compensating for the world's deceitful reward system by taking tranquilizers, alcohol, and drugs? The neighbor of a Christian woman in Las Vegas summed up her final reaction to the hurts and disappointments of her life by saying, "Don't worry, honey, just stay stoned!" Small wonder that the top song of 1988 was that Reggae number, "Don't Worry, Be Happy."

Yet the peace of God is there. Rock steady. Impervious to failure, rejection, outward calamity. Jesus told His disciples that this peace was different. "Not as the world gives do I give to you," He said.[5]

A Time of Turmoil

Think about your conversion to Christ. You probably were in some kind of turmoil. Crisis may have come. Then came a conversation, an evangelistic meeting, a loss of a friend, a financial mess, a gross sin. Perhaps you were sitting alone reading the Bible and the Holy Spirit moved upon you as you realized, "I'm going the wrong way. I'm empty. I need to change."

I remember that unusual moment when I felt for the

first time the peace of God ruling in my heart. My life had become very empty. I knew it, and things were getting no better. I was hollow.

I had been invited to dinner in Philadelphia in the spring of 1956 by an unusual man named Cornelius Vanderbreggen, Jr. After startling me out of my wits by taking a big, black Bible from his handsome briefcase, pushing the dishes back on the table, and placing the huge volume in full view on the table in the very elegant restaurant, he began to talk to me about my relationship with God, which had been under steady but incomplete change for several months.

In return, I told him, "During the past year I've been reading the Bible. At times I think God has talked to me from it."

I paused, waiting to see how my host would react to such an idea. He just smiled, and I pressed on. "I'm convinced God is the only hope for this world." I stopped for a second and then blurted: "In fact, I've decided to enter the ministry!"

Cornelius looked calmly into my eyes. "What do you believe about God?"

My nervousness returned, and I reached for another piece of bread. "I believe He is the source of all power, the guiding intellect of the universe. Not only that, I believe He has a destiny for each man's life, and that none of us will ever be happy or productive unless we are in the center of His will."

Cornelius gave me a quizzical look, but somehow the smile remained. "Pat," he said, "any Mohammedan could have told me what you just said. Isn't there something more?"

I seemed to be speaking in blurts. "Yes, there is something else. I believe Jesus Christ died for the sins of the whole world . . ." I stopped for a second. I knew he expected more, and to my amazement I added five words: ". . . and for my sins too."

I had resisted that moment. But suddenly a Bible verse flooded in my mind: "If you *confess with your mouth* the Lord Jesus and believe in your heart that God has raised Him from the dead, you will be saved."[6] A light turned on within me. I had moved from religion to faith in a specific Person—Jesus Christ. It was as though I had walked through a curtain that had separated me from God. He had answered my yearlong plea: "O Lord, in this life grant me the knowledge of Thy truth and in the world to come life everlasting." I *knew* God.

A smile played on Cornelius' tanned face, but I'm sure even he didn't realize the magnitude of what was going on within me.

The next morning, after Satan hit me with a surprisingly strong attempt to move my mind back to its old course of vulgarity and worldliness, I knew that I was a new person, a new creation as Paul had phrased it.

About three o'clock that afternoon, while sitting at my desk, I leaned back for a moment and burst out laughing. I had passed from death to life, and I was living in an entirely new world. Joy and peace touched every fiber of my being, and the turmoil, the confusion, were gone—displaced.

That was my first experience with God's umpire—peace—and its rule in my heart. I was in the will of God. His plan for my life was unfolding.

Peace Is Your Compass and Gyroscope

This peace becomes your own private compass and gyroscope to keep your life on an even keel. "Let the peace of God rule in your hearts."[7] A more modern translation would render the word *rule* as "be an umpire." The umpire tells you if you are safe or out. The peace of God will tell you whether any words, any actions, any thoughts, any plans are right for you.

A Christian is to be inner-directed by God's peace acting on his or her inner man—the heart or spirit. If the heart is troubled, then the vessel of your life is losing balance and is going off course. If the peace is there, you have one of the most important means of God's guidance, which says, "Full speed ahead!"

We have a slang expression, "I have a feeling in my gut" that such and such is right or wrong. King David wrote in the Psalms, "My reins instruct me in the night seasons."[8] The reins are technically the kidneys, but the concept could encompass the viscera, the gut. "Listen to your gut" may not sound very holy, but if you are a Christian and your innards start to churn, pay attention and get back on course.

Everyone who knows me, knows my fondness for horses. I began riding about forty-seven years ago and since then I have broken horses, trained horses, bred horses, jumped horses, and been on trail rides and fox hunts. I have even owned a small horse business.

In 1982, while I was visiting our television station in Dallas, Texas, I was able to make contact with Jarrell McCracken, the man who had built one radio recording called "The Game of Life" into Word Publishing, the largest religious record company in America.

Jarrell's love in 1982 was not records but purebred, so-called "Straight Egyptian" Arab horses. He had, some years before, purchased for $200,000 a son of the United States Arab Champion, Morific, out of the great Egyptian mare, Moniet El Nefous. This colt, named Ibn Moniet El Nefous, was simply spectacular, and Jarrell was able to syndicate him as a breeding stallion for the then un-dreamed-of price of $4.5 million.

Jarrell sent his ranch's King Air up to Dallas to fly Dede and me to his Bentwood ranch in Waco, Texas. The place had the only stallion barn I had ever seen with an oriental rug in its foyer. There were miles of fences and dozens of beautiful horses, to be precise 70 million dollars' worth of elegant purebred Straight Egyptian Arab horses.

Later Jarrell dropped by our headquarters to discuss some possible collaboration between CBN and Word Records. He also offered me something that it was almost impossible to refuse. His young fillies were bringing up to $500,000 as three-year-olds. Every year they could produce a foal worth $165,000. To own one would be like having a twenty-year retirement annuity. Jarrell knew that I had limited resources, so he was willing to sell me one of these lovely animals for $165,000, with nothing down and the balance to be paid with interest over a four-year period.

To help me, Jarrell would keep the horse, breed it to his stallions, and help sell the foals for me. Since my book *The Secret Kingdom* was a national best seller, it would be easy to pay for the horse and to deduct the entire amount from my income as a business expense.

This arrangement seemed like an incredible deal, but something was wrong. I had no peace in my heart. I could not understand why God would want me to turn down such an opportunity. I kept praying. Still no peace and and a strange uneasiness.

Jarrell called to find out my decision. I said I didn't think I could do it. He in turn sweetened the arrangement even more. I went back to the Lord again. This time He led me directly to the story of Balaam—the hireling prophet who came back to God for a second opinion when a heathen king raised the offer for his services.

Balaam Bargains with God

You'll recall that Israel was moving into the Promised Land. As Balak, the king of one of the threatened nations, saw this vast multitude approaching, he accurately surmised that military might alone would not stop them. He resorted to divination, thinking that a curse would avail more than force of arms. So he sent men to summon the prophet Balaam.

"A vast horde of people has arrived from Egypt, and they cover the face of the earth and are headed toward me," he said. "Please come and curse them for me, so that I can drive them out of my land; for I know what fantastic blessings fall on those whom you bless, and I also know that those whom you curse are doomed."[9]

The messengers from Balak carried a nice diviner's fee with them which they were prepared to pay Balaam. So the prophet told them to spend the night, and he would seek direction from the Lord.

God's reply was specific: "Don't do it! You are not to curse them, for I have blessed them!"[10]

Balak would not take "No!" for an answer. He sent more distinguished ambassadors to persuade Balaam. "King Balak pleads with you to come," they told Balaam. "He promises you great honors plus any payment you ask."[11]

Balaam initially rejected their offer, but then he reconsidered. "Stay here tonight," he said, "so that I can find out whether the Lord will add anything to what he said before."[12]

The prophet should have known that God would not change His mind, but by all accounts Balaam was a rather worldly soothsayer. This time, it appears, he was being tempted by the money, which probably was enough to set him up for life.

That night God told Balaam, "Get up and go with these men, but be sure to say only what I tell you to."[13]

Then, two verses later, the Scripture says that God's anger was aroused because Balaam went with the ambassadors.

What are we to make of this apparent contradiction? First God said, "Don't go!" Then He said, "Go!" Yet He was angry because Balaam went.

The answer seems clear. God first spoke His perfect will to the prophet. But Balaam didn't stick with the first instruction and went back for a second try when the ante was upped by King Balak's ambassadors.

God, knowing Balaam's motives as well as what would take place, let the prophet accompany the men in His permissive will, giving Balaam special instructions, "Be sure to say only what I tell you to."[14]

Still, Balaam had rejected God's perfect will and had been tempted to accept the money. God was angry and He sent an angel with a drawn sword to block Balaam's way. If Balaam had not repented and offered to turn back, the angel might have killed Balaam.

When Balaam arrived at the Israelite encampment instead of cursing the people of God, as King Balak had requested, he spoke a resounding series of blessings. A majestic ending to what could have been a tragedy.

Balaam's story is a frightening example of those who seek personal profit rather than God's perfect will.

Balaam's Mistake Could Have Been Mine

I dropped the Bible like it was on fire. "No way, Lord, will I be like Balaam. There will be no horse deal. Please forgive me for asking." I thanked Jarrell for his gracious offer, but told him that God had said no and that settled the matter.

As the months went by God showed me that He knew a good deal more about the future of the horse market than I did. He also had other plans for my royalties from *The Secret Kingdom*. By the summer of 1983, it became obvious that in order to maintain my personal integrity, I could not move into a residence on the grounds of CBN unless I personally paid for it. Consequently I donated all the prospective royalties on *The Secret Kingdom,* some $300,000, to CBN to pay for the construction of the house that CBN owns but I occupy.

This left me with limited funds and no need for any large tax shelters. A $50,000 payment each year for a horse would have been a terrible burden. In fact, during 1987 and 1988, when I took no salary from any source during the presidential campaign, I would have been financially crippled.

But something much worse happened. In 1986 the market for horses in America started to weaken. Then the Arab horse market crashed. I heard of one horse that might have sold for $10,000 that went for dog meat ($100,000 horses went for $5,000 or less). The big deals were history. The buyers had vanished in a debacle reminiscent of the Tulip Bulb mania of the 1750s.

Bentwood Farms went bankrupt and dispersed their stock; the famous Llamsa Arabians followed suit; Bru-Bet Arabians in Glidden, Iowa, and Scottsdale, Arizona, lost everything. A very wealthy woman I heard of lost her extensive oil, real estate, and bank holdings trying to maintain her Arab horses.

God had spared me from an unnecessary and unpleasant struggle that could have ruined me. He said no, not to deny me but to protect me. And the signal He used was a lack of peace about the decision. His internal guidance system in my life had kept me on an even course, as it will for you if you let it.

9

Practice Humility

In national politics there is a game that all the candidates play called "Managing the Expectations." A candidate may have just received the results of a poll, showing that he is projected to win 60 percent of the upcoming vote, and all his opponents combined will only receive 40 percent. When asked by the press how he is doing, he will drawl, "I feel like an underdog. My opponent, Candidate X, has the most powerful field organization I have ever seen. I am moving in the polls, but I will be delighted with second place."

O course, he knows he has the election on ice, and he is lying right down to the soles of his shoes. If he is able to get away with it, the press will dutifully report that he is an underdog. When he wins, he will be rewarded with headlines proclaiming his smashing "upset" victory. Then he is on to the next state to explain why he is in trouble there and why his opponent is sure to win.

The press makes this type of gymnastics almost obligatory since the press will imply that this same candidate (with a standing of 60 percent) lost the primary if he wins with only 53 percent of the actual vote and his underdog opponent loses with 47 percent. The underdog won, the press implies, because the favorite did not win by as big a margin as was expected.

One rally in Lubbock, Texas, for instance, had a capacity, standing-room-only crowd in a place that seated 2300 people. The local paper reported that 1000 were in attendance. In Dallas, a crowd jammed into a three-story auditorium that seated 4200. The Dallas paper reported 1200 in attendance. In Austin, Texas, however, I had the smallest crowd for any official meeting in the entire state. We set up a luncheon for 180 people but 50 more showed up than expected. We brought in five extra tables. The Associated Press reported that I had such an overflow crowd in Austin that extra tables and chairs had to be brought to handle the people!

Playing the Expectations Game

My problem in the expectations game was twofold. First of all, the expectations game is pure fabrication.

Secondly, the Bible says that a Christian is to "eat well by the fruit of his mouth."[1] That means we confess blessing and prosperity and victory—not defeat and failure. If I thought I was going to win somewhere, I said so! I always encouraged the people who came to hear me to expect victory.

To me, speaking of victory is not arrogance or pride, but an acknowledgment of the power of God. Years ago I met a Church of God minister from Tennessee who said God once told him, "There is no room for retreat or defeat in my program." I did not know how to talk defeat or third place to my supporters, I wanted them to think victory.

The press wondered why I didn't play "expectations." In fact, the ABC producer assigned to my campaign took one of my staff aside and whispered, "When will Pat learn Expectations 101?" The problem was that they did not understand the concept of confessing an anticipated result by faith. What I was saying was nothing but empty bravado they thought.

The expectations game got serious in South Carolina.

I started in the polls in South Carolina at about 4 percent. Three weeks before the primary the polls showed me at 12 to 14 percent, with George Bush at 60 percent. He had the sitting governor and Lee Atwater, the craftiest politician in South Carolina history, masterminding his strategy.

We had sent out a newspaper insert, which simply told what my accomplishments were. My rating jumped from 14 to 28 percent among those who actually read the insert. If all it took was the publication of a few facts to double my rating in the polls, a strong TV campaign could catch the front-runner.

I had to galvanize our South Carolina forces or the rest of the South was gone. So from our New Hampshire headquarters, I said, "Today we played in George Bush's backyard. Now we are going to the South which is my backyard. I throw down the gauntlet to George Bush in South Carolina."

I wanted to move attention away from New Hampshire as quickly as I could and then alert my forces to know that if we didn't win South Carolina on March 5, we could forget the rest of the South on March 8. Instead I alerted everyone else who was afraid I might be on to something. They went after me like hornets.

After New Hampshire, I had about two-and-a-half weeks to get ready for South Carolina and the South. Our people had done extremely well in early state party caucuses. All I needed were eighty thousand votes to win the state, and my state campaign manager had assured me that we had an organization in the state capable of putting the vote together.

Unfortunately, I could not merely concentrate on South Carolina. I had the rest of the South to look after as well, because of a change in the southern primary structure. The Democrats had known that they could not win the general election with a Mondale-McGovern liberal, so they combined the states of the South (where they controlled the legislatures) into one enormous primary. They felt that this Southern vote would force their party to select a moderate candidate. The Southern Republicans pushed the process along, and it was clear in both parties that whoever won the South would win the ball game.

Being a Southerner I felt that a Southern primary would help me, but this type of primary entailed a simultaneous effort in Texas, Oklahoma, Missouri, Arkansas, Louisiana, Mississippi, Alabama, Georgia, Florida, South Carolina, North Carolina, Tennessee, Virginia, Kentucky, plus the state of Washington—an organizational and financial nightmare for a non-political novice.

I decided to organize in all of those states and to wage a contest in them all. I realized that Ronald Reagan was enormously popular in the region, but I didn't realize that George Bush was regarded as Reagan's alter ego in the South. I also did not realize that the Bush forces had been organizing the South for four solid years ahead of the primary.

To top it off, Lee Atwater had arranged to move the South Carolina primary to March 5, so that it would serve as a trigger for their man to set off the big event on March 8.

On one day I boarded our campaign plane in Atlanta at 6:30 A.M. I flew to an airport rally for about seven hundred people in Louisville, Kentucky. Then to a rally for one thousand people in Bristol, Tennessee. Then south to another large rally in Birmingham, Alabama. Then over to a big rally at Mississippi State University. Then up to an airport rally in Kansas City, Missouri. Then over for a rally in Tulsa, Oklahoma and an even larger turnout in Oklahoma City. Finally, to Dallas, Texas for the night.

I was up early the next morning for meetings in Louisiana and a network radio broadcast for an hour, then a brief meeting in North Georgia, and back into South Carolina for more rallies and meetings.

I was told I exhausted the press traveling with me, even some members of the Secret Service. There was no question that I was receiving supernatural strength to accomplish the schedule.

I had never before called on my body and my mind to put out such an effort, and I was always conscious that any slip made before the ever-present press would make unfavorable local or national news.

Be Still and Know, Not Busy and Fatigued

Fatigue feeds mistakes. Pressure builds mistakes. The Bible says, "Be still, and know that I am God."[2] I did not have time to be still. Each day I got up two hours ahead of my departure to pray and read the Bible, but I was just too tired for it to do any good.

My mistakes went up geometrically in relation to the measure of my jet lag and fatigue and the number of press conferences I permitted. It was not by accident that George Bush stopped having press conferences during the general election campaign. He cut his chances for press goofs in half.

Worse than all that, when I got to South Carolina, I was told by our national campaign manager that our money was almost gone. The money drain from the petition campaign finally caught up with us. We then borrowed $350,000 short-term against expected federal matching funds. I taped a thirty-minute television program in a studio in Columbia, South Carolina at one o'clock in the morning. That one broadcast moved my standing in the polls five percentage points, but there were no funds to saturate the state with television advertising.

I took 19 percent of the Republican vote in South Carolina and in so doing improved my preelection standing by five percentage points. George Bush swept the state and I slipped into third place after a near tie with Bob Dole for second.

Had I been relaxed, rested, on television, and out of press conferences, I might have won a clean second.

Clearly, fatigue and pressure can obscure God's will and lead to faulty judgment.

But was "throwing down the gauntlet to George Bush in South Carolina" a reasonable move under desperate circumstances or was it the greatest sin of all: pride?

Pride: The Greatest Sin of All

Absolutely nothing will shut off God's guidance more than pride. Simply put, pride is believing that your plan is better than God's plan. Lucifer, in the first known act of sin in all the universe, said, "I will exalt my throne above the stars of God."[3]

In the early days of mankind, right after the flood, the people said, "Come, let us build . . . a tower whose top is in the heavens."[4] That is, to challenge God. The ultimate form of pride will manifest itself in a worldwide confederacy, much like that at the tower of Babel, when mankind will collectively decide to rebel against God and serve the representative of Satan, a man who in fact will be totally possessed by Satanic power.

- Pride says there is no God.
- Pride says the Bible is not true.
- Pride says we have a theology based on science, and those "myths" are unscientific and not acceptable to intelligent, enlightened people. (Just think, a prideful philosophy called "the Enlightenment" preceded the French Revolution and the Napoleonic wars, which

brought horror to France and much of the continent. People, professing to be "enlightened" and free of the old taboos, said, "Let's remove religion and the church and let man come forth in his native glory and be free of the shackles of God.")

- Pride says God is dead.
- Pride says men can oppress other men.
- Pride says millions of black people can be kept in bondage for one hundred years after abolition.
- Pride says the Aryan race is superior. (Kill six million Jews!)

In a less cosmic sense, pride cuts you off from not only God's advice but the good advice of others. It need not be some monstrous rebellion against God, just the simple statement of a man to his wife, "Thanks a lot, dear. That's a very interesting suggestion, but you don't have the experience in these matters that I do." My wife Dede could probably write a book called *I Told You So* about the times I have refused her advice and made mistakes.

I do listen to her suggestions about some matters, especially when they come from the Lord, but in areas of business and biblical studies and, I thought, politics, my experience and training is superior to hers. In good old-fashioned midwestern common sense, however, she comes out on top almost every time.

When I learned that my campaign in New Hampshire had not been put together properly and I was waiting for word from Mel Thompson to decide to be my campaign manager, Dede said very simply, "That's ridiculous. If Mel wants another candidate that's his business. New Hampshire is a tiny little state. Why don't you get out of it and concentrate on the South?"

The conventional wisdom from most of the "experts," backed up by history from 1952, was that no one could win the general election without first winning his party's primary in New Hampshire. The press attention on New Hampshire, like Iowa, was massive. Those who didn't contend in New Hampshire didn't quite appear to be legitimate candidates. So I said, "Thanks, Honey, but I don't think getting out is possible."

But, oh how right Dede was! Pulling out of New Hampshire before I had become enmeshed in a last-ditch battle I couldn't win would have been the smartest thing I possibly could have done. I would have had at least three more carefully planned weeks of my time to spend in the South, and $1 million more to spend on crucial Southern primaries. I would have been spared the pressure cooker do-or-die attitude my New Hampshire loss forced on me.

God was speaking to me through Dede, but the political "experts" and I knew too much to listen.

Pride shuts out the good suggestions that come to you from loved ones, friends, fellow employees, workers, or supervisors. The key to superior Japanese technology is not creativity. America is far ahead on that front. It is very simply gradual product improvement by hundreds of modifications and innovations. Where do these improvements come from? From the dozens of suggestions that each Japanese worker makes each year in so-called "quality circles."

In America, an adversarial relationship has existed between management and labor, at least until recent days. Management "knew" how to make products. Labor was to do what it was told to do by management. Management's pride shut off such a valuable source of knowledge that eventually many products created in America are now made *only* in Japan.

Pride also brings about an adversarial relationship between you and God. The Bible says, "God resists the proud."[5] In other words, when you set yourself up as a proud know-it-all authority, God Almighty begins maneuvering the artillery of heaven to blow your schemes away. Not to destroy you, but to destroy your false fronts and pretensions so that you finally will come into the blessing of His plan. He does not want any human being to come to the place reserved for the proud: a lake of fire that burns forever, through all eternity.

The reverse of pride is humility. The Bible says that although God resists the proud, He gives undeserved favor to the humble. The seventh key to receiving God's direction in your life is: *Practice humility*. Humility or meekness should be second on the list of attributes that you seek from God, right behind love.

The Humble and the Meek Shall Be Blessed

Think of the privileges of the humble. "The humble He guides in justice, and the humble He teaches His way,"[6] the psalmist tells us. If you develop a spirit of humility, God has promised you that He will lay His plan out before you so that you will absolutely know what steps to take.

What is humility? One of my horses is a fourteen-hundred-pound, sixteen-hand, two-inch German warm-blooded stallion whose name is Aristocrat. I got Aristocrat when he was one year old, and I taught him to work without any lines or restraint. I taught him to "shake hands" and to come when I called him and to back up on command. But he was a big, powerful stallion. One day when he was two, I was leading him into an open pasture. He became frightened and ran away. The rope caught around my finger, and it felt as if he would pull it off. After I caught him and was leading him back, I turned around to see him walking on his two hind legs, towering over me with his front feet poised three feet above my head. He meant me no harm, but he could have killed me.

I asked a Christian friend to train Aristocrat, and later I sent him to advanced training in a discipline known as "dressage." Now he can clear complicated patterns of jumps. He can gallop over a course of four miles while leaping over various obstacles, and he can perform intricate gymnastic feats in a riding ring. He is powerful, athletic, masculine, full of energy, and completely under control. To slow him, all I need to do is gently squeeze my hands on the reins. To stop him all I need to do is suck in my stomach muscles to exert gentle pressure on his back. A slight squeeze with both legs and he trots. A touch with my heel behind the girth and he canters. Pressure by my leg at the girth and he crosses his legs and walks sidewise.

Aristocrat is meek. He has full power, completely ready to serve his master. No fighting. No resistance. No attempt to prove that he has a plan that is smarter than mine.

He trusts me and he obeys me. And I, in turn, have an obligation to feed him, care for him, and to keep him from any situation in which he will be hurt.

I should make emphatically clear that biblical humility or meekness does not consist of a Caspar Milquetoast personality. Biblical meekness is power, authority, bold-ness—all under the control of God.

You and I should become so close to God that all we need is a still voice, a word of Scripture, a chance circumstance, a slight troubling of our peace, or the word of a friend to recognize the guidance of the Father. As soon as the suggestion comes we should be alert to follow His leading—totally yielded, totally trusting, totally surrendered, totally prepared in power and authority. Then we can really begin to experience the miraculous part of His plan for us.

There are two ways to achieve humility: one is voluntary, the other is from the discipline of God's hand.

Voluntary Humility

The biblical command is "Humble yourselves under the mighty hand of God that He may exalt you in due time."[7] You literally are to remind yourself how big God is and how small you are. Then take every opportunity to consciously yield control of the direction of your life to God.

In the mid-1960s, CBN had only one television station and one radio station. Both of them were located in the Norfolk-Portsmouth area of Virginia. I was sure that God was calling us to build a network, but His plan for us was taking an agonizingly long time to come to fruition. I decided to embark on a twenty-four-hour fast on the same day that I was scheduled to speak at a chapter meeting of the Full Gospel Business Men's Fellowship in Goldsboro, North Carolina.

I was in intense prayer during the drive down and after the meeting. The next morning, I was alone, still fasting, in my motel room. As I continued to pray, I found myself saying, "Lord, if you will expand CBN all over the east coast, I will humble myself before you every day, Sunday through Friday, until the victory comes."

I had made a covenant with God. I meant it, and I knew that He had accepted my prayer. From then on for several years I would take time six days of every week to humble myself before God, kneeling with my face down on the floor. I would consciously humble myself before God in surrender to His Will, then I would ask Him to humble me. If I forgot before I left my room, I would seek out a private place where I could kneel and literally put my face on the floor in surrender to God.

This has always been the safest place to be. People might get envious and try to knock down the head of a multimillion-dollar enterprise. They might try to silence a nationwide news network. I have never found anyone who was envious of a man on his knees with his face on the floor in surrender to the Lord.

I lived up to my part of the bargain and God lived up to His. Within ten years of that day of fasting, CBN was not just covering the east coast, it was on the air in some 120 television stations in virtually every major city in America.

Humility from the Discipline of God's Hand

A second way to achieve humility is from God's hand directly. Many times His blessings for us are so wonderful that they cause us to be proud. Unfortunately, every good thing carries with it the seed of our own destruction. Too much knowledge can lead to loss of faith. Too much money breeds indolence and arrogance. Too much acclaim causes us to take our eyes off God and focus them on ourselves.

The apostle Paul received a blessing many long for. He was caught up into the third heaven and saw things that human beings should not see. So that God could continue His plan for Paul, He sent a demon to harass him wherever he went. In the apostle's own words, "And lest I should be exalted above measure by the abundance of the relevations, a thorn in the flesh was given to me, a messenger of Satan to buffet me."[8] God was keeping Paul humble.

God poured His blessings on CBN, and we added five radio stations in New York. Then a television station in Atlanta. Then a concept for a tape network which brought us our first network affiliate, Ted Turner's WRET-TV in Charlotte. Then a network affiliate in Baltimore, than Visalia, California, then Chicago, then Houston, then Dallas, and soon the country.

CBN had become the acknowledged pioneer in a totally new form of Christian broadcasting. People were coming to us from all over the country for help and advice in radio and television. We had formerly lived on cast-off equipment from local commercial television stations.

Now we had a bigger studio and more modern equipment than any other studio in town. We were good, and regretfully we knew all too well that we were good.

But God was not pleased. He had far bigger things for us and because of our sorry attitude He couldn't move us to the next part of His plan.

Our network was exploding with new station growth. Yet our internal cash flow was inadequate for growth so in the late 1960s we began to borrow money by issuing interest-bearing term notes to our donors. Although not a securities specialist, our local attorney assured me that CBN as a nonprofit institution was not required to register these notes with the Securities and Exchange Commission. He did not know that there is an obscure part of the fraud section of the law that requires a full disclosure prospectus even if securities are not required to be formally registered. We paid all the interest on time. We paid all of the principal on time. The affairs were scrupulously conducted. Not one investor was unhappy, because after all, they were Christian people trying to help build a ministry.

Then, in 1974, I read excerpts from the Watergate tapes and publicly called on Richard Nixon to repent. That simple action put my name on the White House enemies list. Within ten days the Securities and Exchange Commission had launched an investigation into CBN's securities. I am convinced that a member of the S.E.C. from California had received a call from the White House to go after us.

And go after us they did. For eighteen months they probed and probed and basically found nothing. But once a government agency gets started, it usually will not stop without some evidence that it was not wasting the taxpayers' money. We were called to account for not issuing a full disclosure prospectus. They faulted us for saying that only money put in God's kingdom was "safe and secure."

In my opinion, we had done nothing wrong. But rather than spend a fortune fighting the S.E.C., we agreed to sign a consent decree under which the issuer of securities neither admits nor denies that he has ever done anything wrong. The S.E.C. permits the operation to continue as before so long as appropriate disclosure is given to past and future investors. The brief agreement then goes to a federal judge who issues a permanent injunction telling the issuer of securities that if he ever does what he has never admitted doing, he will be in contempt of court.

This type of thing is a civil proceeding and not uncommon in the securities business. Unless the party involved has been guilty of some serious breach of the rules, the signing of a consent decree results in no penalties and no substantial changes in procedures. It might rate a small, three-inch column on one of the back pages of the *Wall Street Journal*.

The S.E.C. allowed us to file the consent decree late on a Friday, so the opportunity for any press comment would be reduced. Nothing was said about the decree on Saturday or Sunday or Monday. The matter had been settled, we thought. We were preparing a forty-page prospectus, and the story, we thought, was history.

Then on Tuesday, headlines in the *Dallas Times Herald* read: "CBN Charged With Fraud." Without any corroboration, the United Press picked up the story and ran it to the West Coast. We called them immediately to demand they retract. The U.P.I. Dallas bureau deliberately refused to move a retraction until the West Coast deadlines had all passed and the false story had circulated.

Then the *Atlanta Constitution* ran the same false story under a big headline. Although our public relations people were at the phones all day to answer questions, the *Constitution* reported, "No one at CBN was available for comment."

I was absolutely devastated. I had put this entire matter into God's hands to protect me. We had defrauded no one. No one had lost or would lose a dime. I felt I was the victim of political retaliation for expressing my opinion in 1974. But whatever the facts, the case was closed. Now the press was acting as if a big juicy investigation was just getting underway.

Members of our staff said it must be an attack from Satan. I called a prayer meeting, explained the situation, and told them some inside information I had received about White House involvement. I told them that we were helpless to do anything except pray and ask for God's protection.

Dede and I walked in our front door about six o'clock that evening. I felt disgraced and humiliated and totally drained. I said to her, "God could have protected us. Why did this thing happen?"

I sat down on the hall steps with my Bible in my hand and prayed. At once God spoke to me clearly, *If you want the answer, turn to Isaiah 2:11.*

I opened my Bible: "The lofty looks of man shall be

humbled, the haughtiness of men shall be bowed down, and the LORD alone shall be exalted in that day."

I read it to Dede. "This thing is from the Lord," I whispered. "He wanted to humble us. It will all work out for good."

The humbling took place in the fall of 1975. The exaltation on New Year's Day of 1976. On that day our entire staff walked on the land for our new headquarters building in Virginia Beach. We didn't need to borrow any more money because our income went up almost 250 percent in 1976 over 1975 and we finished the year with $7 million cash in the bank. That year we also started our Satellite Earth Station. The next year we began a cable network that has grown to 45 million households in all fifty states and a graduate university to train the future leaders of the world.

God's plan was right on schedule. I just needed a fresh dose of humility before I could enter into it.

10

Sin Blinds: Get Rid of It

In 1971, I met a most impressive minister from Dallas, Texas, whose name was Ron Blinder.* During the sixties his messages on sin and repentance had led to spiritual revival at his denomination's theological seminary. In fact, he had been one of several ministers responsible for the spiritual awakening of the mother of the general manager of our television station in Atlanta, Georgia.

When I encountered Blinder, he headed a missionary organization in Dallas. The good works of his people were highly regarded throughout the area, so I was pleased to assist him as he endeavored to establish a Christian television station in Dallas, modeled after our CBN stations in Tidewater Virginia and Atlanta, Georgia. A station on Channel 33 in Dallas had gone dark, and I worked out an extraordinary deal with the manufacturer, General Electric, to sell to Blinder and his group the repossessed equipment from that station at about 30 percent of its original sale price. I then introduced Ron to my friend, Bunker Hunt, who loaned him $200,000 in work-

---

*Fictitious name used to protect privacy.

ing capital. Finally, I showed him how to file the necessary papers with the Federal Communications Commission to receive a license to operate Channel 33. Later, I spoke at a fund-raising banquet to help him gain community support.

In short, I handed Ron a station virtually for free that would have given him a fabulous ministry in one of the top ten cities in America and within ten years would have been worth at least $25 million. All he needed to do was continue to follow God's leading, and he would have enjoyed success and the generous support of the community.

But, to the amazement of his staff, Ron Blinder began to program the station with unbelievable trash. On opening day the lead movie was, *I Wonder Who's Kissing Her Now*. No one could believe it, but this man of God seemed to have completely lost any direction for his life. Within the course of a year, his ministry fell apart, his financial support crumbled, and his staff left him. Only a few people remained to program the television station which by now had become an embarrassment to the Christian community in Dallas. I will never forget the words of the station's business manager just before Christmas of 1972: "I think I'll give the people of Dallas a present this Christmas," he told me, "and take this mess off the air."

What happened to Ron Blinder? The answer is simple: In his private life, he fell prey to temptations that blinded him. People engaged in sin make unbelievable errors in judgment. The last key to receiving God's direction in your life is: *Sin blinds: get rid of it*.

Spiritual Blindness

God's clear guidance and supernatural direction require a clear vision of the kingdom of God and a listening ear. The minute that you or I get involved in willful disobedience to God's commands a cloud passes over our spirits. We are like blind men groping for direction without knowing which way to go.

Spiritual blindness is especially difficult for people who have been born again and are accustomed to being led by the Spirit. In the so-called "televangelist scandals," the level of stupidity displayed was so egregious that before it happened no fiction writer would have dared to write about it. Yet, it happened because a succession of acts of sin left those involved blind and helpless.

If a man is born blind (like singer Stevie Wonder), he will learn to adapt from childhood on. In Stevie's case, to become a brilliant composer and star entertainer. But if a person who is accustomed to normal sight loses his vision, the transition can become chaotic.

So it is with spiritual sight. The person who has never been "born again" has never seen the kingdom of God or known what it is to be led by the Spirit. To him, much of the subject matter of this book would seem utter foolishness. These people have developed mechanisms to make judgments, which permit them to function with some clarity. They never see the big picture, and they are never sure of the future; they muddle through day by day.

Their future, however, is not good. Here is the biblical appraisal of the tragedy that takes place in the lives of those who have been blinded by sin:

So God let them go ahead into every sort of sex sin, and do whatever they wanted to—yes, vile and sinful things with each other's bodies. Instead of believing what they knew was the truth about God, they deliberately chose to believe lies. So they prayed to the things God made, but wouldn't obey the blessed God who made these things.

That is why God let go of them and let them do all these evil things, so that even their women turned against God's natural plan for them and indulged in sex sin with each other. And the men, instead of having a normal sex relationship with women, burned with lust for each other, men doing shameful things with other men and, as a result, getting paid within their own souls with the penalty they so richly deserved.

So it was that when they gave God up and would not even acknowledge him, God gave them up to doing everything their evil minds could think of. Their lives became full of every kind of wickedness and sin, of greed and hate, envy, murder, fighting, lying, bitterness, and gossip.

They were backbiters, haters of God, insolent, proud braggarts, always thinking of new ways of sinning and continually being disobedient to their parents. They tried to misunderstand, broke their promises, and were heartless—without pity.

They were fully aware of God's death penalty for these crimes, yet they went right ahead and did them anyway, and encouraged others to do them, too.[1]

If sin blinds us, what then is sin?

The Perversion of God's Plan

One English writer defines sin by telling a parable. One day, he says, you might happen to enter the studio of a famous artist. You walk in and see before you what seems to be a large blank canvas. Paint and brushes are there so you decide to try your handiwork. For several hours you happily splash paint on the canvas, then for a moment you step back and look up. To your horror you realize that you are in the process of ruining a partially finished masterpiece by the great artist.

At its root, sin is the pride which says to God, "I am willing to ruin Your canvas, because I think I can paint a prettier picture than You can in the square before me." The author of the poem "INVICTUS" was a sinner, who wrote, "I am the master of my fate: I am the captain of my soul."[2] Close to home there is a popular song with the same message, "I Did It My Way."

Sin basically comes in three packages: the willful breaking of a known law of God, deliberate iniquity (refusing to conform to the straight standard of God's law), and missing the mark (missing God's target for our lives).

The Willful Breaking of a Known Law of God

King David knew that it was against God's law for him to take another man's wife. He had a heart for God, and yet he was overtaken by his own iniquity and lawlessness, and he made a deliberate decision to sin.[3]

David was walking on the rooftop of his residence in the springtime viewing the beauty of Jerusalem as his soldiers fought a bloody battle with the Ammonites. His wandering eyes landed on a beautiful woman taking a bath, naked, on another rooftop. He looked and he was enticed by her beauty.

He summoned the woman named Bathsheba and committed adultery with her, making her pregnant.

Knowing the shame that would come upon him as king, plus the fact that adultery carried the death penalty, David ordered that her husband, Uriah, be brought home from the battlefield so the forthcoming child would appear to be his.

Uriah, on the other hand, was a noble and valiant man who refused to share the comforts of home while his companions were undergoing the hardships of battle. So to cover that sin, David added another—murder—by ordering Uriah to be posted at the most dangerous point of the battle line and killed.

David had coveted and stolen someone who belonged to another, he had committed adultery, he had borne false witness by lying outright, and he had committed murder.

The light went out in his life. The consciousness of God's presence was gone; his blindness from sin was very nearly total.

Psalm 51 gives us heartbreaking insight to the devastation wrought in David's life by his blindness. "Have mercy upon me, O God," he cries. "Blot out my transgressions. Wash me thoroughly from my iniquity, and cleanse me from my sin."[4]

At one point David states precisely the conditions for returning to the Lord after we sin. They are not to be taken lightly. We are not to sin, confess, sin the same sin, confess, sin again, and so on, over and over, doing what we want to do and now and then turning to the Lord for forgiveness. No, we are to repent, to turn away from our sin, intending to walk blamelessly before God. Here is David's understanding of the matter:

> The sacrifices of God are a broken spirit, a broken and a contrite heart—these, O God, You will not despise.[5]

David had been blinded and deafened by sin. He had lost his way. We can be certain that, had David not returned to his walk with the Lord, he could have made such serious blunders that his nation would have been destroyed.

We need to understand that God provides guidance for us even when we sin. It is called conviction—a work of the Holy Spirit. Although David had begged God not to take the Holy Spirit from him, the fact is that the Spirit was still working in him to bring conviction to his heart. Conviction of sin, then is God's guidance, the Spirit moving the heart to full knowledge of the awfulness of our deeds. The issue is: What will our response be?

God heard David's prayer, and He will hear yours and mine. He reopened the channels of blessing to David. That doesn't mean everything was instantly a bed of roses for him. He still had to deal with the temporal results of his sin, suffering shame, rebellion within his own household, and temporary disgrace in the loss of his kingdom. But he was restored to God, and, really, that's all that matters. God never left him.

Refusing to Conform to the Straight Standard of God's Law

The second type of sin is *the devious quality that the Bible calls iniquity*, which is like a twisting serpent that refuses to conform to the straight standard of God's law.

Did you ever wonder why some little children do such unbelievable things? They lie, they steal, they break things, they have tantrums, they torment their younger brothers and sisters . . . then they become sweet as little angels. The Bible says, "Foolishness is bound up in the heart of a child."[6] This tendency in all of us to be rebellious and do perverse things is part of the nature we all inherit from our long distant relative Adam. The symbolism of Christian baptism is that the old sinful self dies and is buried. Then a new self is formed by the Spirit of God after the nature of Jesus Christ Himself.

Missing God's Target for Our Lives

Thirdly, the Greek and Hebrew words that we translate "sin" actually mean "missing the mark." The image is of an archer launching an arrow toward the bull's eye of a target. The arrow falls short of the bull's eye. Paul wrote, "All have sinned and fall short of the glory of God."[7]

The psalmist makes the rules clear to those who want to live on the mountaintop to see God's plan laid out before them. Anyone who leads a blameless life and is truly sincere, never harms his neighbor, speaks out against sin, criticizes those committing it, commends the faithful followers of the Lord, keeps a promise even if it ruins him, does not crush his debtors with high interest rates, and refuses to testify against the innocent despite the bribes offered him—such a man shall stand firm forever.[8]

A Relationship Not to Be Sacrificed

Since we all do things that are wrong almost every day, what are we to do? The answer is simple. Confess. Repent. Turn away from what we have done that is wrong, and start out again.

The Bible says, "If I regard iniquity in my heart, the Lord will not hear."[9] You know what you have done wrong. If your heart is dead and cold, and the sky seems like brass . . . if there is no leading from God, then you know something is wrong. Find it—confess it—and put it away. The mistakes that may ruin your life just aren't worth the sin involved.

One night when I was on the air at our television station in Dallas (yes, in 1973 we put Channel 33 back on the air and later moved it to new facilities as Channel 39, KXTX-TV), a caller reported a serious accident involving one of our employees, an engineer. The message was that she was in critical condition at Parkland Hospital. My general manager and I drove the short distance up Harry Hines Boulevard to the hospital.

When I arrived and asked to see the young lady, the attending nurse gave me a peculiar look and then said it wasn't possible because the patient was unconscious. We negotiated for a bit, then finally I exploded, "Look, I am a clergyman and by right you must let me see this girl."

To which the nurse replied, "Do you know why she is here?"

"I thought she had been in an accident."

"No way!" the nurse barked out. "She had O.D'ed on drugs. But go on in. I can't stop you."

There, unconscious in the intensive care, was a little slip of a girl who didn't look as if she weighed more than one hundred pounds. I laid my hands on her head and prayed for her, then left.

Only several days later did I find out the full story. The young lady was a born-again Christian, working for CBN, a Christian ministry. Yet she developed a physical attraction for a young man and they began living together. Her Christian life was going down the drain, and she began to hate herself. She wanted to end the relationship, but she felt she loved the young man too much to break it off. She was torn between her love for her human lover and her love for the Lord.

By now, she was receiving no clear direction from the Lord other than a guilty conscience and the loss of her peace and joy. In her blindness she decided that the best way to end her dilemma was suicide. So she swallowed a huge dose of pills and almost lost her life. No romantic affair is worth the sacrifice of a human life. As I later discovered, harboring bitterness is not worth our relationship with the Lord.

Post-Campaign Bitterness

After the Republican Convention in August of 1988, I was requested to be one of the surrogate speakers for the Bush campaign. I campaigned throughout Ohio, in parts of Kentucky, Pennsylvania, Texas, Louisiana, and North Carolina, with brief semi-political visits to Michigan and Illinois. It was easy work. All I had to do was point up the failings of Mr. Bush's ultra-liberal opponent to the party faithful and the press.

Then, to my relief, it was over. On election night, before the vote was all in, I called George Bush in Houston to congratulate him on the big win. As usual, he was most gracious. In a few hours, he was the president-elect.

And I was back into the work of CBN. On the air, I was saying the same things as two years before. Yet, our audience and our staff knew something was missing. The love affair between "The 700 Club" hosts and our audience was legendary. Now, the comments coming from the mail and the telephone were all too often mean, vitriolic, and suspicious. In thirty years I had never encountered anything like it.

I was praying for long periods in the mornings and on Sundays. I was searching the Scriptures as seriously as ever, but that sweet communion that I had known with the Lord before the campaign just wasn't there. I knew that He was with me, but it was as if my life was on autopilot. God was surely flying the plane, but I didn't know where He was.

The one thing that I had told Him I would not give up to run for office was gone, the most precious thing in the world: my relationship with the Lord Himself.

As 1988 came to a close, I prepared myself for an annual prayer retreat to seek God's guidance and direction for the coming year. I stayed at home away from the telephone and began to pray.

Then, a terrible thing began to happen. Every time I started to pray one of the hurts that I had suffered during the campaign would flash into my mind. I am a former

Golden Gloves heavyweight boxer, and, to my amazement, Pete McCloskey would be opposite me in the ring where I could get at him to pay him back for what he had done to me.

I would think of letters to write to the publisher of *The Washington Post* to call him into account for turning over his national wire service as a vehicle for an irresponsible reporter who distorted my resume and tried to humiliate my family.

I drafted letters in my mind to a so-called "Christian" columnist who alleged with irresponsible falsehood that CBN had spent millions on my campaign. Then, I calculated the cutoff days for initiating a libel suit against the Newhouse newspaper chain, which had carried column after column by this same man calling me Elmer Gantry and worse.

I remembered the headline on the upper right-hand front page of the *Des Moines Register:* "Robertson Linked to War Prostitutes." Here was a hearsay rumor dating from thirty-seven years before. This wasn't journalism but a last ditch attempt by a partisan newspaper to hurt me politically.

And there were many more . . . playing through my memory . . . evoking a response . . . disquieting my spirit.

I knew that the Bible says to pray for my enemies. I tried to do that one by one. I thought of ways to do good to those who had spitefully used me. It did not work. Something had hooked me and I couldn't shake the hook loose.

I shared what I was experiencing with my wife, Dede. We prayed together. I knew that time was a healer and perhaps the passage of time would heal these scars that had built up in my memory.

Then came New Year's Eve. Dede and I invited my son Tim, his wife, Lisa, and Lisa's parents, David and Barbara Nelson, who were visiting from Denver, Colorado, for a special dinner at a little restaurant that is a favorite of mine, LaBroche. This delightful occasion left me feeling much encouraged about the new year.

Dede and I got home for a ceremony that we had kept on New Year's Eve for some thirty-five years. There was a crackling fire in the fireplace and a bottle of sparkling cider and the two of us alone. We wanted to ask God what He had for us and for our children for the new year.

We prayed. Then Dede said, "I have a word from the Lord for you." She handed me her Bible, and I began to read the words of the apostle Peter:

> Beloved, do not think it strange concerning the fiery trial which is to try you, as though some strange thing happened to you; but rejoice to the extent that you partake of Christ's sufferings, that when His glory is revealed, you may also be glad with exceeding joy. If you are reproached for the name of Christ, blessed are you, for the Spirit of glory and of God rests upon you.[10]

As I read those words, it was as if God Himself was speaking to me. A deep peace began to enter my heart.

Dede smiled, "It says that you are supposed to rejoice over what they did to you. So be happy."

I laughed, and then said jokingly, "That's well enough for you to say. Remember it was me that they were writing about, not you."

Then, she gave me a little book by a dear lady that I had once met in Darnstadt, West Germany, Mother Basilea Schlink, founder of the Evangelical Sisters of Mary. The book was entitled *The Hidden Treasure In Suffering*.

Mother Basilea had written that of all the suffering we can endure, slander is the worse. It is worse than physical sufferings because it cuts to the spirit and leaves lasting spiritual scars. It is possible to get over a beating, but how does a person get over the loss of his reputation?

But Mother Basilea went on and I paraphrase: These wounds are from the hand of a loving Father who would make you more like His Son. Don't try to fight against them with the means of your old carnal self. Rather, receive them as a blessing from God.[11]

Tears welled up in my eyes. There would be no grudge fights, libel suits, or harsh letters. What I received was evidence that God's Spirit rested upon me. I was free, with a deeper anointing of God's Spirit than I had ever known.

Instead of wanting to fight the ones who had mistreated me, I needed to thank them. They were God's instruments to lead me to a higher understanding of His love and power.

PART THREE

---

*His Direction Today
and Tomorrow*

11

He Sees the Future

I returned to New Orleans in July of 1989 to speak at a Fourth of July God and Country rally in Jefferson Parish for five thousand people.

As I got off the plane from Norfolk, I was met by a friend from New Orleans named John Rondeno. John had been a pillar of strength both during the campaign and at the Republican Convention. I hugged him with genuine warmth.

On the way to the Riverside Hilton in downtown New Orleans, he turned to me with a sly grin and said, "Did you get the news about the Republican central committee?"

"I heard a little," I replied. "Tell me about it."

The story was exciting. Three vacancies had developed in the governing body of the Louisiana Republican party. Speculation was rife in the state legislature as to which public officials would fill the post. But when the meeting was held, all three posts were filled by what are called "Robertson" people.

I asked John how it had happened. "It is simple," he replied. "We elected fifty members of the central committee during your primary."

"Do you have any allies?" I asked.

"There are thirty-six conservatives who vote with us, and that makes a majority of the membership. Besides," he chuckled, "our people always show up and our leader, Billy McCormick, always has a game plan. By the time the opposition gets over their headaches from the night before, the votes are over and we've won."

The next day a member of the Louisiana state senate visited with me at the hotel and confirmed John's report. He was a former Democrat who had recently switched parties when he saw the strength for pro-family, pro-morality issues that my supporters had brought to the Republican party.

He chuckled, "After that central committee vote it is obvious who has the final say in the party." He was planning a race for the United States Senate and realized that our dedicated people in Louisiana could virtually guarantee the Republican nomination if they decided to support him.

The story from Hawaii is similar. Our people swept 82 percent of the caucus vote in that state and sent a pro-Robertson delegation to New Orleans. A member of the legislature of Hawaii came to visit our campaign headquarters to invite me to visit the Aloha state. "There have been only two evangelical Christians in the Hawaii legislature," he told me. "For ten years I have been unsuccessful in getting Christians to run for public office. After your campaign, we now have one hundred and seventy people willing to try."

My Texas director, Richie Martin, remarked after the primary there, "Brother, you know that Jesus talked about a grain of wheat falling onto the ground, then dying and later bringing forth much fruit. What happened in this election is simple. You went into state after state and died. Now the seed that you planted is bearing much fruit."

The Fruit of My Candidacy

Could it be that the reason for my candidacy has been fulfilled in the activation of tens of thousands of evangelical Christians into government? This campaign taught them that they were citizens with as much right to express their beliefs as any of the strident activists who have been so vocal in support of their own radical agenda at every level of our government. For the first time in recent history, patriotic, pro-family Christians learned the simple techniques of effective party-organizing and successful campaigning.

Their presence as an active force in American politics may result ultimately in at least one of America's major political parties taking on a profoundly Christian outlook in its platforms and party structure.

I have always known that a dedicated coalition of evangelicals and pro-family Roman Catholics hold in their hands the absolute majority of votes necessary to insure that the occupants of many seats in the House of Representatives, in the Senate, and, of course, the White House itself, would be men and women who hold a biblical worldview. If the Congress and the legislatures and the judges impose laws and decrees repugnant to Christians, the 100 million or more Christians in America only have themselves to blame.

In August of 1986, at the crucial straw ballot in Ames, Iowa, I expected third place and was given first place. I had nothing to do with the victory. It was all done by the staff and the people. Yet, in the reception to celebrate the victory, those wonderful people were congratulating me.

Then one lady came up to my wife Dede with tears in her eyes. "Thank you," she said, "for letting us have a voice in our government again."

If my candidacy gave millions of people a voice in their government again, my effort was worth it. But was that God's total plan?

In the New Testament we read that Jesus received constant criticism from the people in His society who were not His disciples. "A holy man—a rabbi," they said, "should not be seen eating and drinking with tax collectors and prostitutes." They called Jesus a "wine bibber and a glutton."[1]

Jesus said (and I paraphrase), "You don't like us happy and you don't like us sad. Nothing seems to please you, *but wisdom is justified by her children.*"[2] In other words, let's withhold judgment until a man's words and deeds have a chance to grow up. As you watch the long-term effects of what is done, then you will know whether the present action was wise or foolish. So it is with my campaign.

The "children" of my campaign have not yet grown up. When they do, we all will know whether their presence in American public life was God's reason for leading me to enter the race.

I followed God's leading for my life in this race. As I have pointed out in this book, I made mistakes. But none of the mistakes were fatal because in my heart I only wanted God's will and His plan for me, His plan for His church, and His plan for the United States of America. What I did was carried on with honor and integrity according to the wisdom that God made available to me.

CBN Today

I returned to CBN wiser and stronger than ever in my life. After God set me free from the lingering bitterness and wounds from the campaign, I have seen a renewed sense of spiritual power that is as great as I have ever known. God has anointed me with "fresh oil." The miracles taking place day-to-day in this ministry are instantaneous, dramatic, and awe-inspiring.

Our CBN staff is smaller, but there is extraordinary harmony and unity. We all sense a literal explosion of creativity and effectiveness. Our mission is in clear focus. We are working better, smarter, and more efficiently than ever before. In 1989 our goal for numbers of people won to Christ exceeds that of any year in our history. We are building an International Conference Center so that people from America and all over the world can come to find God's plan for their lives. Next year we launch in four nations of Central America the most comprehensive evangelistic blitz in the history of that region. We expect two million decisions for Christ in that region alone next year.

My absence from our flagship television program "The 700 Club," caused a sharp drop in audience. When that was coupled with the so-called televangelism scandals that rocked the nation, CBN's income from contributions dropped more than half, plunging by a staggering $75 million per year. Yet God was not surprised by the revelation of wrong-doing in other ministries—this was judgment that He had planned for years to prepare His church for a great revival. He obviously was not surprised that I left CBN to run for the presidency. This was His call and clear direction, planned before the foundation of the earth.

A Man Named Abraham

Almost four thousand years ago God tested a man that He had chosen named Abraham. God had promised Abraham that he would be the father of a multitude—in fact his descendants would be as numerous as the sand of the sea. Abraham waited, but no seed came. The promise from God never dimmed in Abraham's consciousness. He did not give up hope even while he watched his body gradually shriveling and his sexual potency diminishing as he approached the age of one hundred and his wife Sarah the age of ninety. The Bible tells us that he "who, contrary to hope, in hope believed,"[3] that through his seed all of the nations of the earth would be blessed.

Then a miracle happened. A son that they called

"laughter" was born to them. A son of promise. A son who was to fulfill all of the promises of God to Abraham and to a waiting world. The most precious son in all the world.

But when Abraham's son, Isaac, was barely in his teens, God called on Abraham to test him. "Abraham," God said, "will you take your son—your only son—up to Mount Moriah and sacrifice him to me?"

Abraham was shocked beyond measure. This request defied reason. How could God promise something to him all his life, finally give it to him, and then take it away? How could God in one stroke destroy His entire plan to bring redemption to all mankind? How could God frustrate His promise to Abraham to give him and his seed the promised land? We can imagine Abraham thinking, *Why, God, are you so arbitrary? Why, God, are you so cruel? Why me, God?*

Whether Abraham entertained these thoughts we can't say, because the record is silent. What we do know is that he went forward with Isaac and a bundle of wood to Mount Moriah to give to God the ultimate form of human surrender—the sacrifice of the most precious thing in his life.

But when the fire was laid under the altar and his only son was bound on it and Abraham's hand holding the knife was plunging toward Isaac's heart, God shouted out, "Abraham, stop!"

As he held back his hand and looked around, Abraham saw a ram caught in a thicket. He had passed the test of ultimate obedience. He had become a very type of God himself who would one day two thousand years later offer His only son as a sacrifice for us all on Mount Calvary. With a heart filled with gratitude and relief, Abraham untied his son and drew him close. Then the two of them sacrificed the ram to the glory of Jehovah God.

As Abraham contemplated the miraculous last minute provision of the Lord, he breathed in a prayer of thanks, a new name for God, Jehovah Jireh, the Lord "my provider." The root of the Hebrew word that Abraham used does not mean "provide" but "see" or "choose." What Abraham was saying was that while he was walking up one side of the mountain, Jehovah his God was seeing the other side of the mountain and was choosing an appropriate sacrifice to bring forward at just the right time. God "provided" for Abraham's need by seeing ahead and then preparing in advance a sacrifice which was placed before Abraham when it was needed and where it was needed.

In short, God is not taken by surprise when His people follow His plan. In fact, He has "seen" ahead and begun the preparation to meet our need long before we realize that we even have a need.

God's Provident Plan for CBN

In 1977, God saw that in ten years I would be leaving CBN for a time and that a financial crisis could develop for the ministry that we both loved. God was testing my obedience as He tested the obedience of Abraham, but He had no plan to kill my "Isaac," only to refine it.

So in 1977, He led us to build the first satellite earth station ever owned by a Christian ministry. Then he led us to rent for ten years a little transmitter (called a transponder) on a satellite that was in orbit 23,000 miles above the equator. For the first time CBN would be able to transmit "The 700 Club" program live across America. We could save taping costs and foreign expense associated with the program. Now we could really get serious about up-to-date news coverage.

I signed a contract with my friends at the RCA Americom Company for exclusive use of a transponder on their SATCOM III-R Satellite. Home Box Office bought the first ones. Ted Turner bought next. CBN was third. On April 29, 1977, there was a ceremony beginning our service. To me it was fulfillment of the words of Revelation 14:6: "I saw another angel flying in the midst of heaven, having the everlasting gospel to preach to those who dwell on the earth."

A new era had begun for CBN. What I did not realize then was the provision that God had seen over the years that would come from this humble beginning.

Soon we realized that cable systems in smaller towns across America were looking for programs and would be able to receive them from our satellite transponder. So as an experiment we began to send up six hours of religious programs, repeated four times a day for a twenty-four-hour service. One man, Scot Hessek, was responsible for the entire service. To my complete amazement, after about two years this rather primitive service was carried twenty-four hours a day by cable systems having 5 million subscribers.

Scot Hessek came to me and said, "This thing is getting too big for me to handle alone. I need help."

"Finances are a little tight," I told him, "but we can let you hire a secretary." So with 5 million national subscribers in place, CBN Cable doubled its entire staff, from one to two.

To me the satellite was still a big microwave in the sky to take out programs to broadcast stations. I went along because the economics of the thing made sense. God knew the vast potential of cable and quietly nudged us into it. He had a plan for me and for CBN, and He was looking ahead to provide for us.

By 1981 the number of cable homes for CBN Cable was about 19 million, but not too many people were watching. Only the most dedicated Christians will watch back-to-back preaching repeated four times a day. Our television stations in Norfolk, Atlanta, Dallas, and Boston were all operating as family-oriented, fully competitive commercial television stations. In the setting of wholesome family entertainment was placed "The 700 Club" and other religious programs. The concept worked wonderfully. The secular programs drew large audiences to our stations. The large audiences drew advertisers who helped pay the bills. The religious programs could speak to much larger audiences than would have been available to an all religious station, and commercial revenue paid most of the bills, making a much smaller demand for contributions.

It was obvious that what I had been learning since 1973 in our broadcast stations was right for cable, so we began an interesting, competitive program mix on cable. In 1983 I brought my son Tim to our headquarters from a stint of managing our Boston station, WXNE-TV, in order to take charge of the CBN Cable Network. In that first year under his leadership, the audience watching CBN Cable went up 300 percent—an industry record. God had been training me, training Tim, training CBN for what He would do.

By 1987, CBN Cable was received by over 41 million households in the United States. And today, more than 45 million households are projected to receive CBN. Gradually, advertising revenues from CBN Cable were moving up—from $20 million to $30 million to $40 million to $60 million to $75 million. By our fiscal year 1989, the revenues from Cable had surpassed for the first time the revenues received from contributions.

And to my amazement, the surplus profits from CBN Cable in 1988 were not only sufficient to create bold new programs for Cable, but were exactly what we needed at CBN to pay our bills and still show a little surplus.

Without those funds—and they totalled millions of dollars—CBN would have been forced to retrench to such a degree that we may never have recovered. With those funds we doubled our giving to Operation Blessing, added back fifty new broadcast affiliates to our program line-up, began broadcasting again on the government-owned station in Communist Nicaragua, and started construction of a Conference Center.

Hopefully by 1990, our level of contributions will be moving back to what is needed to sustain the ministry. But whatever happens, I can say a prayer of fervent thanks to the God who sees ahead and provides for His plan.

The Ultimate Outcome

A presidential campaign is brutal. The president of the United States is the chief executive of a vast bureaucracy and a budget in excess of $1 trillion. He sets policies that mean billions of dollars to businessmen, bankers, investors, labor unions, and foreign governments. He is commander in chief of the armed forces and his finger rests on the nuclear button.

Therefore, the press of this nation will ruthlessly drill any newcomer who gets near all that power.

Some perceived me as a threat and set out to do me in. The technique was simple. Merely distort every statement. Leave out key details. Belittle the size of crowds and popular support. It got so bad that one of my supporters cried out, "Lord, when will you vindicate your man?" But God's vindication does not necessarily come during the short space of an election cycle.

After it was over, I asked myself a simple question: "If God called Jesus of Nazareth to be the Messiah, why did He fail?"

But you would say to me with the wisdom of almost two thousand years of hindsight, "Jesus didn't fail!"

You and I know that Jesus was part of God's perfect plan. The apostle Paul wrote, "When the fulness of time had come, God sent forth His Son."⁴ Jesus was born at a time of Roman peace; of universal Roman roads and commerce; of one major language; and at a time when all other religions were in critical trouble. He was born at the precise moment that Christianity needed to begin. At the very moment when in God's plan the world setting was deemed perfect to bring to all mankind the message of God's salvation.

But Jesus of Nazareth did not live in the flesh to see God's message spread throughout the known world. Jesus of Nazareth did not become king of Israel. Jesus of Nazareth did not deliver his people from Roman rule. Jesus of Nazareth led no armies. He established no governmental program.

In fact, by every contemporary human standard, Jesus of Nazareth was a misguided idealist who was crushed by His own nation's religious leaders acting in league with the Roman governor. He was tried by a court of law and was executed by the authorized government authorities. He died, was placed in a tomb, and He left behind a handful of brokenhearted followers.

The prophet Isaiah describes it this way: "He is despised and rejected by men, A Man of sorrows and acquainted with grief, and we hid, as it were, our faces from Him. It pleased the Lord to bruise Him."[5]

But Jesus rose from the grave! His Spirit came in power upon His downhearted disciples. His followers ultimately took control of the Roman Empire. Some three hundred years after the time of Jesus' death, Constantine, the Emperor of the Roman Empire, peaceably accepted the lordship of Christ, bringing the empire with him.

Was Jesus Christ following the will of God? Of course He was. Was He hurt in the process? Terribly so. Was the hurt in the plan of God? Yes, for the Bible says, "It pleased the Lord to bruise Him."[6] Will He ultimately be vindicated? Gloriously so. The Bible says, "Therefore God also has highly exalted Him and given Him the name which is above every name."[7]

After two thousand years has Jesus finally been vindicated? To those who believe in Him, absolutely. To the world, not yet. He is still waiting the ultimate vindication of God's plan for the world when every eye shall behold Him crowned "King of kings and Lord of lords."

God had a plan for Jesus Christ. You might ask, does God have a plan for you and a plan for me? Absolutely . . . a plan every bit as perfect in its timing as God's plan was for Jesus Christ. Will God's plan for you and me always bring immediate worldly wealth and success? No, but God's plan will always bring peace and joy and fulfillment. Our duty is to find His perfect plan for our lives and to follow it with the ability He gives us. It's His responsibility to bring about the results.

I know that something wonderful happened as a result of my run for the presidency. I know that God not only provided signs and guideposts for the race that were unmistakable, His hand of blessing after my return to CBN has been so strong that it can only be interpreted to say, "Well done, my son. You have been faithful, now receive My blessing."

The week before the Super Tuesday primary I flew into the Bristol, Tennessee, Tri-Cities airport for a rally. There were about one thousand people in that early-morning crowd—shouting, clapping, waving banners. After a brief speech, I walked across to shake hands with the people.

One member of that big crowd lives in my memory—a

little tow-headed, freckle-faced boy about ten years old. He looked up at me with eyes full of trust, and as I shook his hand, said, with all the earnestness he could muster,

"PLEASE WIN!"

To him I must reply, "Son, I don't know your name, but I want you to know this. I followed God's plan for me, so in His eyes I did win. And you, too, can always be a winner, if you just put your hand in God's hand and walk on down the road with Him."

Address of M. G. "Pat" Robertson to the National Convention of the Republican Party New Orleans, August 16, 1988

Four years ago the keynote speaker at the Democratic National Convention told us that America was a tale of two cities—the haves and the have-nots. The rich and the poor. The upper class and the lower class.

We heard a variation on that message from Jesse Jackson and Teddy Kennedy and every Democrat who spoke last month at their convention in Atlanta.

Ladies and gentlemen, the time has come for truth. The message of the Democratic Party is a message of defeat—division—and despair. They did not speak for the American people under McGovern or Mondale or Carter, and they do not speak for America today!

But that speaker who compared America to *A Tale of Two Cities* was right in a way he never intended.

That great novel by Charles Dickens begins with a double sentence: "It was the best of times. It was the worst of times."

In 1980 Ronald Reagan and George Bush began a long journey to rescue this country from the "worst of times." From double-digit inflation—soaring interest rates—and widespread unemployment.

As Republicans, our task in 1988 is to continue that journey and build the greatness of America through moral strength.

Exactly two months and twenty-two days from tonight some one hundred million of our fellow citizens will go to their polling places to choose the future course of the United States of America.

Our tale of two cities is really a choice between two paths. Two visions of America. Two philosophies of the future.

When Charles Dickens wrote his epic novel, he described in heartrending detail the consequences that the right and wrong choices made on two cities in Europe.

In city number one, under the deceptive slogan liberty, equality, fraternity—the people with revolutionary zeal threw out God, the church, established morality, the established government, their former leaders, sound currency, and some of the private ownership of property. Then they demanded that the new government buy them happiness.

Instead of the government-inspired utopia which the people thought they would get, they got liberal divorce laws and a breakup of families, anarchy, looting, ruinous inflation, and financial chaos.

As the madness fed on itself, they got something much worse—the reign of terror. A time when no one's life was safe from the dreaded guillotine.

The second city followed a very different course. There, faith in God was maintained. There was even a spiritual revival under John Wesley. Respect for the rule of law prevailed. Instead of wild excess, there was self-control and self-restraint. The currency was strong and families were stable. Private property was protected and life was held sacred. With all its faults, England created a strong, stable conservative government that survived with prosperity for a hundred years.

And so, these two cities made choices in 1789 that shaped their future for decades, for generations, to come. And now, 200 years later, America faces its choice.

The Democrats have given us a clear picture of their city. They offer unlimited government, massive transfers of wealth from the productive sector of society to the non-productive, and ever-increasing regulation of the daily lives of the people and their children.

In the city of the Democratic Party, the liberal mindset reigns supreme. Criminals are turned loose and the innocent are made victims. Disease carriers are protected and the healthy are placed at great risk.

In the Democrat's city, welfare dependency flourishes and no one is held accountable for his or her behavior. Society is always to blame.

In the Democrat's city, the rights of the majority must always take a backseat to the clamorous demands of the special interest minorities. And yet, in their city it is always the majority that must pay the bills, through higher and higher taxes.

Now the Democrat Party has discovered the family. They want us all to be *one . . . big . . . family*. But let's keep in mind that they want you and me to be in one family with Jim Wright as the daddy, Barbara Mikulski as the momma. And Teddy Kennedy as big brother. I can't speak for you, but I believe I'd rather pick my own relatives.

To build their city, the Democratic Party has selected Michael Dukakis as architect. I submit to you tonight that Michael Dukakis is the most liberal candidate ever put forward for the presidency by any major party in American history.

In fact, the city the Democrats hope to build is so bad that they are ashamed to mention the word that describes who they are and what they really want to do. They don't want to say it, so they just call it the "L" word.

They know that their programs will require massive new revenue, but in their platform they did not mention once the vehicle they will use to raise the money—they just call it the "T" word.

Whether by silence—whether by initials—or whether in a foreign language—it's still tax-and-spend liberalism and the American people are too smart to fall for it again.

There is another word that the Democrats did not mention once in their platform and not once in the acceptance speech of their candidate. It is a "G" word. The name of God.

Ladies and gentlemen, our President, Ronald Reagan, was not ashamed to ask the assembled delegates at our convention in Detroit to bow their heads in silent prayer to God. As Americans, we are not ashamed to pledge allegiance to a flag that is a symbol of one nation under God.

And I submit to you that our party, the Republican Party, assembled here in New Orleans, is not ashamed to write into our National Platform our solemn resolve that the children of this country will once again be allowed to pray to God in the classrooms of America.

As an aside, I should mention that Michael Dukakis is a card carrying member of the A.C.L.U., an organization dedicated to removing all public affirmation of religious faith in America. As President, Michael Dukakis will pack the federal courts with A.C.L.U. radicals. If there were no other reason, and there are many, to deny Michael Dukakis the presidency, this is a reason enough for all of us to vote against him in November.

Ladies and gentlemen, the Republican Party wants to write a tale of another city.

We are the children of those who tamed the wilderness, spanned a continent, and brought forth the greatest nation on the face of the earth. We are the heirs of those who enriched the world with the electric light, the telephone, the airplane, mass-produced automobiles, the transistor, and countless wonderful inventions.

Yet we are the heirs of a more enduring legacy than mere material progress. We are heirs of a legacy of ideas —a legacy of freedom—of equality—of opportunity. A legacy of government of the people, by the people, and for the people. We are the heirs of an experiment in freedom that has given hope and promise to all of the people on this earth.

We see a city set on a hill. A shining light of freedom of all of the nations to see and admire. A city made great by the moral strength and self-reliance of her people.

A city where husbands and wives love each other and families hold together.

A city where every child, whether rich or poor, has available to him the very best education in the world.

A city where the elderly live out their lives with respect and dignity, and where the unborn child is safe in his mother's womb.

A city where the plague of drugs is no more and those who would destroy and debase our children with illegal drugs are given life sentences in prison with no chance for parole.

A city where the streets are safe. Where criminals are locked up and the law-abiding can walk about without fear.

A city where the water is pure to drink, the air clean to breathe, and the citizens respect and care for the soil, the forests, and God's other creatures who share with us the earth, the sky, and the water.

A city with limited government but unlimited opportunity for all people.

We are Republicans and we believe in government that is our servant, not our master.

We believe that the wisdom of the millions who make up the marketplace is greater than the wisdom of the few who serve in government.

We want a balanced budget, but we believe the way to balance the budget is to cut waste and mismanagement in government, not to raise the taxes on the American people.

There is a word to describe us. It is a "C" word. We are conservatives and we are proud of it!

In November the voters will choose their version of *A Tale of Two Cities.*

Some people say that they don't care what choice the voters make in November. That it doesn't really matter.

I say to you tonight, *We care because it does matter.* It matters to us and our children whether we vote Democrat or whether we vote Republican.

And we care whether the successor to a great President, Ronald Reagan, is a liberal who returns us to the failed policies of Jimmy Carter or a principled conservative like George Bush who moves us proudly into the nineteen nineties.

Etched in my mind is the memory of a forty-year-old black man. He was strong—he was honest—he was hardworking—he was handsome. He was a family man with a wife and a couple of children.

He was building a place for himself and his family—when one day tragedy struck him.

You see, he couldn't read and write. He had been running a loading dock for a fertilizer distributor. He got along by memorizing the colors of the products that he handled, until the company changed the labels, and he made so many mistakes that they had to let him go.

His life is now in shambles. His pride is gone. His hopes and dreams are gone. He is one more on the welfare rolls. He is one of the thirty million functional illiterates in America who have been shortchanged by our educational establishment.

Ladies and gentlemen, George Bush wants to be known as the "Education President." Together we can make our schools the best in the world if we follow a few simple steps:

1. We must guarantee to our children a disciplined, drug-free, crime-free school environment. Tough school principals should be made community heroes not community scapegoats.

2. We must recognize that the so-called New Age curriculum of progressive education is a colossal failure and must be replaced.

3. We must place control of education in the hands of

parents and teachers in the local communities and take it away from Washington, the federal courts, and the liberal leadership of a powerful teachers union.

4. We must give to every parent the maximum freedom to decide what school is best for his or her child. Empowering parents with vouchers and educational choice at the state and local level is an idea whose time has come.

Yet some would say, we can never have better education without stronger families.

In part they are right. In my opinion the breakup of the American family is the number one social problem in our nation today.

Half of our marriages end in divorce. Over fifteen million children now live with a single parent. According to press reports, over half of the women with children in the black community do not have any man in residence.

Single women with children are the fastest growing segment of the poor in our land. We speak of the feminization of poverty.

But what has government done about the problem?

Successive Democratic Congresses have raised the tax burden on parents with children an estimated 245 percent over a twenty-year period.

In one year federal taxpayers' money was used to institute an estimated 225 thousand divorce actions.

It has been estimated that 30 percent of all divorces in America are caused by misguided welfare laws.

More cruel than all this is the assumption begun by Lyndon Johnson's Great Society programs that the poor did not have to strive, to learn, to compete, to excel.

This attitude fostered dependency, then hopelessness, then despair.

Ladies and gentlemen, we are Republicans and we believe some basic truths:

1. Government must seek to strengthen families, not tear them apart.

2. Parents are responsible for their own children. If a man fathers a child, that child is not the responsibility of the city, the state, or the federal government. That child is his responsibility, and he and the child's mother should be made to look after it.

3. Women in our society should have complete access to challenging and rewarding careers. If women in our society do the same work as men, they should receive the same pay as men for that equal work.

4. We also need to stop punishing women in our society who choose to be homemakers. If in our society we can afford to give tax deductions and credits to working women with children, we also can afford to give tax deductions and credits to women who want to stay at home and care for their children.

5. The goal of welfare must be to restore people in crisis to dignity and useful employment . . . not to create a class of government dependents for whom welfare is a way of life. Whatever the Democrats may tell you, that is *not* the way to "keep hope alive."

But hope *is* very much alive in America today. It is alive because our vision, the Republican vision, expresses the hopes and the dreams of the vast majority of the American people.

And, as we leave New Orleans, we will go back to our

homes confident that we are a party united around a platform that expresses the American spirit—a platform we can be proud to share with our neighbors all over this great nation.

Now I would like to give a personal, special message to the millions of voters, volunteers, and supporters across America who committed themselves to my campaign. I thank you. I am very proud of you. Now the time has come for you to make your choice.

This party is about to nominate a man that I have come to respect and admire.

This man can and will lead our nation proudly into the future.

Therefore, tonight I release my delegates and alternates who have come to this convention and urge you and all of my friends across America to give your enthusiastic support to our party, our candidates, and our presidential nominee George Bush.

As we cast our eyes toward November, we know that a new page of history will be written.

On that page we will inscribe the name of the forty-first president of the United States.

His name will be George Bush, Republican.

Thank you and God bless you!

Notes

CHAPTER 1

Did I Miss It?

1. Garry Wills, *Time*, 21 November, 1988.

CHAPTER 2

You Are Somebody

1. Isaiah 58:7–11.
2. *Ibid.*
3. Isaiah 58:11.
4. "Religion in America," *The Gallup Report*, Report No. 236, May 1985, 50–51.
5. *Ibid.*
6. Jeremiah 1:5.
7. *Ibid.*
8. *Ibid.*
9. Dorothy Sayers, *The Man Born to Be King* (Gollanez, England: David and Charles).
10. Corrie ten Boom, *Tramp for the Lord* (Old Tappan: Revell, 1974), 11–12.
11. Psalm 30:5.
12. 1 Peter 1:8.

CHAPTER 3

Believe That God Will Guide You

1. Matthew 7:6.
2. Hebrews 11:6.
3. Acts 7:22.
4. Romans 8:28 (TLB).
5. 1 Kings 22:34.
6. See 1 Kings 22:30–36.
7. Psalm 127:2.

8. John 3:2.
9. John 3:3, 5.
10. "My Sweet Lord," George Harrison (Hollywood: Capitol Records, Inc., 1970).
11. 1 Corinthians 2:9–10.
12. Psalm 25:7.
13. John 8:29.
14. Exodus 26:30.
15. Matthew 6:10.

CHAPTER 4

Surrender to His Will for You

1. John 7:17.
2. Ephesians 2:10.
3. Luke 10:17.
4. Luke 10:20.
5. Matthew 7:23.
6. Matthew 7:21.
7. Luke 12:47–48.
8. See James 3:1.
9. Acts 26:19.
10. See Proverbs 4:2.
11. Exodus 3:1.
12. "What's Ahead for Pat Robertson?", *Saturday Evening Post*, March 1985.
13. Judges 6:11.
14. See Judges 6:11—7:25.
15. Isaiah 29:17–18.
16. Romans 11:33, 36.

CHAPTER 5

Practice God's Will Every Day

1. Matthew 25:29.
2. Hebrews 5:14.
3. Romans 12:2.
4. Matthew 6:10.
5. Micah 4:2, 3.
6. Isaiah 28:10.
7. Brother Lawrence, *The Practice of the Presence of God*, trans. by E. M. Blaiklock (Nashville: Thomas Nelson, 1982).
8. Matthew 28:20.
9. Ephesians 2:10.
10. Tal Brooke, *When the World Be As One*.

11. Genesis 2:9.
12. *Ibid.*
13. Genesis 2:16–17.
14. 2 Corinthians 3:17.
15. Projections based on data from the Alan Guttmacher Institute.
16. Statistics provided by American Social Health Association.
17. National Clearinghouse Alcohol and Drug Information, P.O. Box 2345, Rockville, MD 20852.
18. Taken from the 1989 Surgeon General's Report.
19. National Clearinghouse Alcohol and Drug Information, P.O. Box 2345, Rockville, MD 20852.
20. Study published by the *Journal of the American Medical Association*, July 1989.
21. Hebrews 5:14.

CHAPTER 6

Look for Two or More Witnesses

1. Matthew 18:16.
2. See Acts 10:1–46.
3. Malachi 3:6.
4. Ephesians 2:10.
5. Joshua 3:10 (TLB).
6. 1 Kings 18:24 (TLB).
7. 1 Kings 18:36.
8. See 1 Kings 18.

CHAPTER 7

Know the Bible

1. Matthew 9:17.
2. Hebrews 1:1–2.
3. 2 Timothy 3:16.
4. Exodus 20:14.
5. 1 Corinthians 6:18.
6. Exodus 20:13.
7. Exodus 20:15.
8. Leviticus 18:22.
9. See Malachi 3:8.
10. Malachi 2:16.
11. Ephesians 5:25.
12. Ephesians 5:22.
13. John 16:13.
14. John 10:35.

15. Galatians 1:8, 9. (Italics used by author for emphasis.)
16. See Hebrews 12:14.
17. Romans 12:19.
18. See Hebrews 12:14.

CHAPTER 8

Let God's Peace Be Your Umpire

1. Colossians 3:15.
2. John 14:27.
3. John Bartlett, *Familiar Quotations* (Boston: Little, Brown, 1982), 540.
4. Matthew 10:12–13.
5. John 14:27.
6. Romans 10:9.
7. Colossians 3:15.
8. Psalm 16:7 (King James Version).
9. Numbers 22:5–6 (TLB).
10. Numbers 22:12 (TLB).
11. Numbers 22:16–17 (TLB).
12. Numbers 22:19 (TLB).
13. Numbers 22:20 (TLB).
14. *Ibid.*

CHAPTER 9

Practice Humility

1. Proverbs 13:2.
2. Psalm 46:10.
3. Isaiah 14:13.
4. Genesis 11:4.
5. 1 Peter 5:5.
6. Psalm 25:9.
7. 1 Peter 5:6.
8. 2 Corinthians 12:7.

CHAPTER 10

Sin Blinds: Get Rid of It

1. Romans 1:24–32 (TLB).
2. John Bartlett, *Familiar Quotations* (Boston: Little, Brown, 1982), 663.
3. 2 Samuel 11:4.
4. Psalm 51:1–2.
5. Psalm 51:17.
6. Proverbs 22:15.

7. Romans 3:23.
8. See Psalm 15.
9. Psalm 66:18.
10. 1 Peter 4:12–14.
11. Mother Basilea Schlink, *The Hidden Treasures in Suffering*.

CHAPTER 11

He Sees the Future

1. See Matthew 11:19.
2. See Matthew 11:17, 19.
3. Romans 4:18.
4. Galatians 4:4.
5. Isaiah 53:3, 10.
6. Isaiah 53:10.
7. Philippians 2:9.

www.ingramcontent.com/pod-product-compliance
Lightning Source LLC
La Vergne TN
LVHW030634080426
835508LV00023B/3353